Praise for
How to Be Your Own Genie

*"Radleigh Valentine has penned a fun, inviting, enthusiastic, and very special
book. He deftly manages to weave angels, wish fulfillment, manifesting your best
life, and personal stories (some poignant, but most hilarious) with glitter, love,
and a heartfelt honesty and integrity that's so refreshing in the spiritual self-help
world. You will smile through it all and remember who you really are. When
you accept his invitation to Genie Academy, you'll learn that life is magic, you
are magic, and there is nothing stopping you from living your best life! Bravo,
Radleigh, for sharing your fabulous joy and miracle-making secrets with all of us!"*

— COLETTE BARON-REID, best-selling author, oracle expert,
spiritual medium, and founder of Oracle School

"Radleigh Valentine's new book How to Be Your Own Genie *is brilliant! It
not only shows you how to release the magic inside of you and how to use it in
all areas of your life but also helps you understand and know that the genie has
always been there . . . you just needed to wake it up!"*

— JOHN HOLLAND, medium, spiritual teacher,
and author of *Psychic Tarot for the Heart*

*"This ingenious book will help you take the cork out of your bottle and release all
your inner blocks to happiness, success, abundance, inspiration, and love."*

— ROBERT HOLDEN, author of *Shift Happens!* and
co-author with Louise Hay of *Life Loves You*

*"Joymaster Radleigh Valentine is the perfect guide to show you how to claim
the truly magical life you were meant to live. If you feel your light has gone out
or that you're stalled in manifesting your dreams, this book will show you how to
wave your own personal magic wand and let the miracles flood in! I found myself
laughing and nodding big yeses all the way through this book. I'd say to keep it by
your bedside for an instant dose of joy and inspiration any time you need it!"*

— JEAN HANER, author of *Clear Home Clear Heart:
Learn to Clear the Energy of People and Places!*

"If there's a spiritual road map for life, this is it! You'll never need to buy another self-help book; everything you need is in this gem of a book. You will learn how to embrace joy . . . and release everything else. With a light and open heart, **Radleigh Valentine** gently and graciously guides you through life's meandering path with sage advice and a depth of love. Highly recommended!"

— DENISE LINN, best-selling author and founder of the International Institute of Soul Coaching®

"**Radleigh Valentine's** book is pure magic. It is quirky, fun, and most of all illuminating. If you are ready to grab the wonder in life, this is the book for you!"

— DIANA COOPER, best-selling author and founder of the Diana Cooper Foundation

"**Radleigh Valentine** has created a powerful and easy-to-use tool to help you unlock and reclaim the magic in your life. Radleigh not only wrote the book on this important subject, he lives it every day. This book is a fun, empowering read."

— GRANT AND MELISSA VIRTUE, authors of *Angels of Love*

"When is the last time you did something that would take you closer to a life that you'd love? Well, read How to Be Your Own Genie, and you'll receive a roadmap that will lead you to the path of your greatest dreams. You deserve happiness and love, and you deserve to achieve your goals. However, it's so easy to get distracted by everyday life. Let **Radleigh Valentine** teach you how to make powerful changes that will get you back on track and keep you there.

"Radleigh has filled this book will insightful exercises that will help you get clear on your goals, release blocks, and commit to a life of joy—all sprinkled with a healthy dose of sparkly magic that only Radleigh can deliver! The guidance here is timeless, and I know you'll be referring to this book again and again. So grab your magic carpet and join Radleigh as he takes you on a wonderfully transformative journey to awaken your inner Genie."

— ROBERT REEVES, N.D., co-author of *Nutrition for Intuition* and *Angel Detox*

HOW TO BE
YOUR OWN

Genie

ALSO BY RADLEIGH VALENTINE

BOOK

The Big Book of Angel Tarot

CARD DECKS

Animal Tarot Cards

Fairy Tarot Cards

Angel Answers Oracle Cards

Guardian Angel Tarot Cards

Archangel Power Tarot Cards

Angel Tarot Cards

All of the above are available online and
at your local bookstore. Please visit:

Radleigh's website: www.RadleighValentine.com
Hay House USA: www.hayhouse.com®
Hay House Australia: www.hayhouse.com.au
Hay House UK: www.hayhouse.co.uk
Hay House South Africa: www.hayhouse.co.za
Hay House India: www.hayhouse.co.in

HOW TO BE YOUR OWN

Genie

MANIFESTING THE MAGICAL LIFE YOU WERE BORN TO LIVE

RADLEIGH VALENTINE

HAY HOUSE, INC.
Carlsbad, California • New York City
London • Sydney • Johannesburg
Vancouver • New Delhi

Library of Congress Cataloging-in-Publication Data

Names: Valentine, Radleigh, author.
Title: How to be your own genie : manifesting the magical life you were born
   to live / Radleigh Valentine.
Description: 1st edition. | Carlsbad : Hay House, Inc., 2017.
Identifiers: LCCN 2017044299 | ISBN 9781401951313 (tradepaper : alk. paper)
Subjects: LCSH: Magic. | Jinn.
Classification: LCC BF1621 .V35 2017 | DDC 133.4/3--dc23 LC record available at
   https://lccn.loc.gov/2017044299

ISBN: 978-1-4019-5131-3

10 9 8 7 6 5 4 3 2
1st edition, November 2017

Printed in the United States of America

SUSTAINABLE
FORESTRY
INITIATIVE

Certified Sourcing
www.sfiprogram.org
SFI-01268

SFI label applies to text stock only

FOR SAMMIE

CONTENTS

INTRODUCTION

Life Is Magic!

You. Are. Wonderful.

That's right—you heard me. I said you're wonderful. Amazing. Beautiful. Okay, maybe a little quirky, but only in the *best* of ways. You're funny, but also thoughtful. *Brilliantly unique.* Frankly, you're a miracle. And I adore you.

Now, when was the last time you heard someone say that to you? Ideally, it would have been this morning when you got up! It should have been the first thing you said when you looked in the mirror.

I know, however, that it can be a little difficult to feel special. After all, by the last count I read, there are 7.5 *billion* people on the planet. And it can seem like all of them are on Facebook, Instagram, Twitter, or Snapchat—or all of the above. You're constantly being informed of the planet's mind-blowing accomplishments. Meanwhile, you're busy raising kids while holding down a job and trying to maintain your body in some form of health. Your schedule is so packed that it's difficult to find the time to squeeze in any mind-blowing accomplishments of your own.

Or so it might seem . . . in your perception, anyway.

Keep in mind that each person on the planet *is* unique and special and amazing. While you may agree with this statement on a certain level, I know agreement is often followed by whispers in your mind that say: *Well. Except you. Everyone is special* except *you.*

I know that voice. It's called the ego. I, too, have succumbed to the shackles it can bind you with to keep you from discovering happiness. There was a time when I was certain that my dreams were completely out of reach.

But then something happened . . .

I discovered that life is magic!

The change didn't happen overnight. Slowly but surely, I came to realize that there is magic not only in the world but also in *me*.

And then I was free.

BORN "DIFFERENT"

I was born *different.* Just writing that sentence makes me laugh out loud because it's such an understatement. In fact, as my wonderful mother passed over into Heavenly bliss, her last words to me were, "Having you as a son has been . . . *different.*" While for some people that could have been a distressing thing to hear, I assure you that my sister and I thought it was hilarious, simply because it was so undeniably true!

Still, being different didn't feel very funny as a kid. Nor did it continue to be amusing for the first 30 or so years of my life. To be honest, if I could have avoided autobiographical information in this book, I would have happily done so. But I've been told by the best editors in the world that I can't merely *tell* you that life is magic; I have to *show* you. So I guess that makes my life my own "exhibit A"!

I'm 100 percent perfectly clear on my purpose in life, and part of that is to show you that life really *is* magic! That *you* are magic! And by following the philosophies of this book, you can completely change *your* life just as surely as I did mine.

So just how different was I? Well, I had my first psychic experience when I was five years old. I awoke in the middle of the night, looked out my bedroom window, and saw my best friend dying. If you're wondering what's so strange about that, it was *impossible* to see my friend's house from my bedroom window. I alerted my parents, and they took immediate action. Sadly, the ambulance got lost, and my friend passed away.

For weeks, I wouldn't set foot in my bedroom. Eventually, my mom took my hand and led me back upstairs. We then sat on my bed while she explained that what I had was a special gift and I shouldn't be afraid of it nor should I ever doubt it. Even though my first psychic experience was so traumatic, I'm thankful that I had a very understanding mother to guide me through the confusion.

Another thing that makes me unique is that I'm part Native American on both my parents' sides; two of my great-grandmothers were Cherokee. I believe that our ancestry has an effect on us that is always present, even if we aren't always conscious of its impact. The sound of tribal music always has a powerful effect upon me, even if I just hear it in passing such as in an airport.

I wrote my first "I love you . . . do you love me?" note when I was six years old *to another boy*—effectively outing myself in the first grade. On top of that, I grew up in a part of the United States where this event affected my social life by making me essentially friendless until high school, so I withdrew into a world of imagination and science fiction. And when I went to college, I "accidentally" wound up with an accounting degree.

Put that all together, and we get a psychic, part–Native American, gay, nerdy certified public accountant.

What?! Do those descriptors even go together?

Apparently so.

To further complicate my life, my absentee father, when he was around, was emotionally and sometimes physically abusive. As you might imagine, I liked it best when he was just absentee.

However, as I mentioned before, what I did have growing up was the most amazing mom in the world and a wonderful sister. My extended family unfortunately lived rather far away, so that meant my childhood largely consisted of just my mom and sister, an alarming collection of Legos, and some pretty cool dogs.

I also had some unique psychic gifts that God had blessed me with and an awesome guardian angel named Joshua.

THE RECOVERING CERTIFIED PUBLIC ACCOUNTANT

After surviving high school, I left my small hometown as quickly as possible for a very nice college. Adding to the evidence that the Universe has an ironic sense of humor, I didn't fit in at that college any more than I did at home.

Like many college kids starting out, I wasn't at all clear what I wanted to do with my life. I majored in music and dance, switched to psychology, then moved on to business classes. By the time I "woke up" to what was happening, I was so far into a business major that I was trapped. I ended up finishing school with that "accidental" degree in accounting. People who knew me were shocked. (But not as shocked as I was!)

I like to call myself a "recovering certified public accountant," but that's mostly just a joke. (*Mostly.*) Being an accountant wasn't really all that bad. Whether I was happy or unhappy was based solely on *whom* I was doing the work with. If I liked my peers and co-workers, then I was fine. If I didn't, I was miserable.

What couldn't be denied was that the work wasn't "me." At the time, though, I had no idea what being "me" might actually look like. That started to change in my early 30s, when I felt pulled to explore my spiritual gifts more thoroughly. Organized religion didn't feel safe to me, yet I had a deep need to express my spirituality in some way. For me, that meant delving into the realm of angels.

In retrospect, my natural gravitation toward angels makes sense. Although I didn't know it at the time, my guardian angel Joshua had been making "appearances" in my life from the age of five. I now know that it was Josh who woke me that sad day when my friend left this Earth. And Joshua's presence was particularly notable in my late teens and early 20s as I wrestled with my identity. At that point in my life, I knew there were angels, but I hadn't officially met Joshua. I hadn't even made the link in my heart and mind that there were guardian angels specifically dedicated to me. But when I was 20, I fell in love for the first time. This nine-month romance had a powerful effect upon me. When it ended, I was devastated; I was sure I'd be alone for the rest of my life. While crying my eyes out, I suddenly heard a voice that I'd later come to recognize as Joshua's, saying, "You are not going to be alone." A wave of peace came over me, and I stood up knowing that I was going to be okay.

After my first "happy job" as an accountant ended, I wound up in a miserable job. I believe now that this was Heaven's first attempt at shaking me loose from the idea that I was going to be an accountant forever. The miserable job led to another happy job, but that eventually ended too and led to another, even *more* miserable job.

Still, during this time, I continued to study spirituality. I started flexing my psychic muscles in receiving Divine guidance from above, and I began to do intuitive readings for friends and family. I discovered that I was very, very good at it. I discovered the tarot and became fascinated with it. (My study in tarot began 30 years ago and continues to this day.) I also came to realize that genuinely helping others by doing readings for them filled me with absolute joy! I felt like Harry Potter suddenly realizing magic was real.

Then I discovered this publishing company called Hay House and fell in love with their books and authors. I took courses with their teachers and, somewhere along the way, realized that it had become my fervent dream to *be* one of them.

I wanted to be a spiritual teacher and author . . . but instead I was a *certified public accountant*.

Hey, no problem! This should be a simple transition, right?

You know what? Actually, *it was.*

My spiritual path awakened in me a knowing that everything that happens is leading us *somewhere*. When we follow our Divine guidance, then that "somewhere" is a happy place. When we allow fear and worry to guide our steps, then suddenly that somewhere *isn't* so great a place.

I came to understand that Heaven *wanted* me to be happy. God was always pushing me toward joy, even if it didn't feel like it at the time. I had discovered the magic that was within me and its connection to the Divine. I knew that *I* had the magic necessary to make my wishes come true.

And so do *you*!

Your Invitation

Your life is meant to be one of wishes granted and dreams come true, and you have the magic within you to make that happen.

So what that means is . . . you can *be your own Genie*!

Now, I want to take you on a magical journey. I'm going to share with you all I have learned about manifesting happiness, the career of your dreams, and true love. I'm going to introduce you to the Genie that lives within you and show you how to use your magic to have the life you've always wanted.

My name is Radleigh Valentine, and I'm living a magical life. I would like to invite you to live there with me.

— Chapter 1 —

Your Inner Genie

Life is magic. Seriously, it really is! It permeates everything you see, feel, and care about. This fact is completely obvious to people living a magical life. But there's no need to worry if it's *not* so obvious to you, because I can teach you to "see"! The first step is recognizing that inside of you is a magical manifesting energy, which I call your "inner Genie."

You might have noticed that I capitalized the word *Genie.* Well, that was on purpose. After all, we capitalize the word *God*— which, not so coincidentally, starts with the same letter as Genie. Whether you prefer to use *God, Divine, Source,* or *Universe,* all these words basically express the same concept: We are all connected. We're all a part of God, and there's a little bit of God in all of us.

This magic within you, the part of yourself that allows you to live a very magical life, is the bit of God within you. In other words, your direct connection with the Divine is the Genie energy!

In this chapter, I'm going to explain how to access your inner Genie, as well as what might have blocked your ability to successfully work with the magic within you . . . until now.

WHAT IS MAGIC?

I've chosen to live a magical life. But what does it mean to live a magical life, exactly, and what am I referring to when I use the word *magic*?

When I say "life is magic" or that there's magic flowing through all of us, I'm talking about that same energy that connects us all. My experience of that energy is one of total joy! It's one of infinite opportunities and the ability to create the life you want to live.

We often think of magic as being the *big* things that happen in our lives. Sometimes it is! But like a tiny snowball rolling down-hill, gaining speed and size as it travels, the magic in our lives most often starts with little things that turn into much bigger pieces of our "dreams come true" as time goes by. Magic shows up when we come to *believe* in it.

Everything that everyone does on planet Earth has powerful importance. The key is not necessarily *what* you're doing . . . but how you're *perceiving* what you're doing.

Some people say perception is reality. I get that. I agree that how we perceive the world in many ways determines the kind of world we wind up living in. But magic is also brought to life by per-ception. For example, you might see coincidences as charming but not really noteworthy. You may view kind words that come from a stranger as nice but of no great consequence, even if you desper-ately needed to hear them. You might barely register signs from Heaven, like white feathers or pennies on the ground or butterflies —and even if you do notice them, you may think, *So what?*

Instead, I would urge you to look upon those things as magical interludes from the Universe. Clues that you're on the right path. Hints that your needs are noticed and provided for. Messages that you're loved.

Having a magical life is intertwined with, and inseparable from, faith. It comes from *believing* that you're meant to be happy and *knowing* that you can make your dreams come true. Having a magical life requires having trust that you're on a Divine path meant to lead you somewhere amazing.

It also means believing in the Genie that's within you, just waiting for you to start making wishes.

When it comes to having a magical life, I take nothing for granted. I look for meaning in *everything* that happens. Sometimes that meaning eludes me. My longest search for the meaning of something that had happened to me took eight years. And yet, in all that time, I never stopped doubting that there was a purpose behind the experience I'd had. When the meaning did eventually present itself, I realized that it had been one of the most important things that had ever happened to me! It might be tempting to think that the longer you wait for the meaning, the bigger the meaning is, but *big* meaning can also come in an *instant.*

When you're constantly paying attention to what the Divine has to offer you, the magic of life becomes impossible to miss. When you believe that everything (and I do mean *everything*) in your life happens for the sole purpose of bringing you nearer to God and to a life of joy, then happiness finds *you!*

However, not everything is about you. Sometimes you'll get the opportunity to play a part in someone else's magical moment. For example, I might see, hear, or be a part of something that doesn't seem to have magical meaning to me, but my presence in that moment might make the magic mean something to someone else. Because I'm so in tune to the magic of life, I often find myself explaining to other people the miracle of something that just happened. Just a case of right time, right place? Simply a coincidence?

Or did Heaven put me where I could help someone else see the magic?

Here's an example: Not too long ago, I was talking to a friend while we walked along a busy street. She agonized over whether or not she should quit her job in order to follow her dream of opening her own bakery. As she explained all the pros and cons of taking such an action, I suddenly noticed a billboard across the street. I started laughing uncontrollably and pointing at the sign, which said "Just do it!" My friend had been standing with her back to the billboard and undoubtedly would never have noticed it had I not pointed it out to her. That was a magical moment that had absolutely nothing to do with me. I was just there to bring her attention to that magical message from Heaven.

These moments prove to me that the Divine is working through my inner Genie to help make wishes come true. I *believe* in magic, so life allows me the blessed opportunity to spread it around.

BEWARE THE EGO TRIP

Perhaps the biggest block to accessing the inner Genie is the ego. When I use the term *ego*, I'm referring to the part of your mind that works at cross-purposes with you. It's the aspect of your consciousness (and sometimes the subconscious) telling you that you're not good enough. That somehow you're not worthy of happiness, success, or a magical life.

Your ego causes you to second-guess yourself and doubt your ability to accomplish the things you wish to create in the world. It tries to convince you that you're separated from God and cut you off from the magic of the Universe that's meant to be your birthright. It's the nagging voice you hear in your head that says you're not pretty enough, you're not skinny enough, you're not funny enough, you're not smart enough . . . you're just not *enough*.

I don't know about you, but I'm seriously considering contacting an attorney about getting a restraining order on my ego. You know . . . something along the lines of: My ego can't speak to me. Must stay at least 50 feet away. If it accidentally shows up at the same place I'm at, then it must vacate the premises immediately.

I mean, wouldn't that be super cool? But, alas, your ego is sewn to your steps much like Peter Pan's shadow. Wherever you go, it's there, too.

In its own little way, the ego is trying to help; it's not trying to be mean. It thinks it's protecting you from disappointment, sadness, and emotional or physical harm. But what it really does is keep you from the happiness that comes from being able to access the magic of life. It's as if it's constantly running around with a shovel, trying to keep your knowledge of your inner magic buried.

One of the things that can define how much power your ego has over you is your childhood. If your parents were fearful or anxious people, that same negative energy may have been programmed into you. In their desire to love and protect you, they may have reinforced the unfortunate influence of your ego over your life. Perhaps, in their desire to push you to be successful, they frequently pointed out characteristics of yours that they perceived as being "not enough." You may have taken their critical words to heart, instilling your tendency to listen and believe the negative thoughts of your ego.

But you mustn't believe it! When your ego tries to tell you to act like an adult or that you're not good enough or that magic doesn't exist in the world, do what I do. Stick your fingers in your ears and say, "Lalalalalalalalalalala!"

The ego hates that.

The Infinite Infant

In order to truly awaken and empower your inner Genie to create things that make you happy, you have to realize you have the power within you. However, most people aren't in touch with that part of themselves. Similar to the "inner child," which refers to the playful and carefree aspects of you that may be hidden from your consciousness, your inner Genie is the part of you that's connected to the magic of the Universe possibly without your being fully conscious of it.

There's a reason why I related the "inner child" with the "inner Genie." Our ability to create magic in our lives is at its most powerful when it arises from a place of joy, purity of intention, and belief. These qualities come naturally to children. We arrive in this world innocent and trusting, fully expecting our needs to just magically be taken care of. As children of the Divine, we're infinite examples of love, or "infinite infants"!

Part of having control of your inner Genie is being in touch with your infinite infant. You deserve to have all your needs met in a joyful and uplifting way throughout your entire life!

The ego will try to convince you that everyone in the world is special and magical—except you. Getting in touch with your inner Genie will erase that false notion from your mind. Your magic is unique to you, and getting to know it will remind you that *you* are indeed special. *You* are amazing. There's no one else like you, and therefore the world needs you to be as fully authentic as possible, regardless of what anyone else thinks.

Because . . . you are *wonderful*.

Take Control of Your Habitual Thinking

Getting in touch with your inner Genie requires being awake to the ego. It necessitates being in control of your thoughts, because they are, in essence, the wishes you're making.

Thoughts are powerful things. The thoughts and feelings that we focus our attention upon dictate the experiences we have. Unfortunately, the daily chatter from the outside world, as well as our own inner dialogue, tends to focus on the things that we perceive to be wrong or not going the way we want them to. We spare only momentary notice to the *wonderful* things that happen every single day—if we give them any notice at all.

Thus, negative thinking becomes a habit. We're told that life is not fair, so expecting the worst becomes second nature. We're expected to give up our dreams and belief in magic in favor of careers that make us unhappy just so that we adhere to society's expectations of success.

Think for a moment about how often you anticipate that something won't go the way you want it to. How often are you right? It's a lot of the time, isn't it? Wow, you must be pretty darn psychic! (Well, you *are*, but that's not my point here.)

You often expect things to turn out contrary to your liking—so they do. You're tapped into the Genie within and don't even know it, yet that inner Genie is working very diligently. Your anticipation or expectation is a *wish*. Even when you dread something, it means that you expect/wish for a negative outcome, which the magic of the Universe duly provides.

See? The magic *is* real! The trick is to turn that energy around so that your inner Genie is granting happy wishes instead of unhappy or fearful ones. Once you get control of your thoughts, you can start using them to weave magic in your life in a way that brings you joy.

Your emotions also have the power to direct the flow of magic. However, your emotions are almost always just a reflection of your thoughts. So when your thoughts are negative or in a depressed state, your emotions will follow. I call this the "corkscrew effect." The more negative your thoughts, the more that corkscrew grinds downward, taking your emotions with it. When your thoughts and feelings are both in a negative state, the magic that happens is quite unpleasant.

To remove a corkscrew, the process must be reversed. In this case, that means you must first focus your efforts on uplifting your emotions so that you can then work on your thoughts. (We'll talk more about that in Chapter 4 in the section called "Happy Magic.")

BREAK FREE FROM THE COMPARISON TRAP

One of the ways in which you lose control of your thoughts is through comparing yourself to other people. To demonstrate why this is the case, I'd like to share something that happened to me right after graduating college.

My first job as an accountant was with an amazing publishing company in a Southern city. It was hands down the best place in the city to work—if not the entire state. To have the opportunity to work there was an incredible blessing, and I was lucky enough to be hired straight out of college. I still look back upon that time with fondness.

Not too long after I began working there, my boss and mentor hired a very talented woman by the name of Glenna. Although I had started working there before Glenna, she had more experience than I did. I found myself weighing my successes against hers and holding the recognition I got for them up to the standard of her achievements. Because I was younger and inexperienced,

I found myself always feeling as though I was just behind her. Never quite measuring up. In short, I was comparing myself to Glenna at every turn.

Well, let me tell you, my ego had a field day with that! I created a great deal of turmoil for myself (as well as for my boss) by indulging in my insecurities. It also placed Glenna and me in an adversarial relationship. At some point, I finally realized that comparing myself to Glenna was making me severely unhappy. I was using my connection to the magic of life only to create upheaval, damage to my self-confidence, and unnecessary drama.

When I finally stopped this unhappy practice, Glenna and I grew very close. She became one of my very best friends in the world at the time, and to this day she is someone I look upon with great respect and admiration.

If you're going to compare yourself to someone, compare yourself to who you wish to be. Then use your Genie magic to make the wish to become that person come true.

MAGICAL LIFE 101

To get in touch and have a fantastic relationship with your inner Genie, there are a few basic principles that you need to understand. The following are concepts that you need to accept and integrate into your life to move forward through this magical guide. (Don't worry—I'll be explaining each of them in much more detail in later chapters.)

Each is a skill like any other, a little like going to the gym. (Don't groan.) All I'm saying is that you start small and build up. But if you can harness the faith, your power will grow really, really fast!

1. The first principle is to **stay awake**. I'm serious. You have to be awake . . . aware . . . paying attention! It's important to notice each moment and everything that happens, with one eye trained to look for a magical message. You might find it, or you might not. (As I said before, not everything is about you. Sometimes

you're just standing in to help with someone else's magic.) But the more you pay attention, the more you notice, and the more magic comes your way! It might take effort at first to stay awake, but in a very short time it just becomes natural.

2. The second thing to do is to **give up the concept of coincidences**. There aren't any coincidences, only *synchronicities*. While they may *seem* like coincidences, they're actually little magical events that are meant to be like messages in a Genie bottle just for you! Don't ignore them or wave them away. Note if something happens that makes you go, "Whoa! That was weird!" It probably wasn't just an odd event but, instead, Heaven trying to tell you something.

Synchronicities happen all the time as a way for the Divine to help you out. Think of them as bread crumbs leading you on your path toward joy. The more you pay attention to them and give them credence, the more they'll happen!

Here's an example: Recently, some friends of mine were trying to make a decision about where to go on vacation. The mom wanted to take the kids to the beach, but the dad had been thinking that the kids were the perfect age for a trip to Walt Disney World. They were discussing the pros and cons as they got into their car to run some errands, and when mom turned on the ignition, a commercial for Disney immediately played on the radio.

Now, you might think, *Huh. That's an interesting coincidence.* No! That's a synchronicity. That's a message from Heaven saying: "Take the kids to Disney! You'll have a blast!"

3. The next principle is to **be aware that people, and their presence in your life, are magical**. Have you ever met someone and just instantly had a strong emotion toward them? If you think that's no big deal or has no deeper meaning, then you're missing something amazing. Sometimes you meet someone and your heart just does a little jump! This can lead to romance, but it doesn't have to. I knew the moment I met my friend Dan that his coattails were lined with magic. The first time I met my dear friend Doreen Virtue, she took my hand to say hello and neither

of us could let go. Whether you feel an instant like or dislike for someone, be sure to pay attention.

You should also know that the Universe, if you ask it to, will send you mentors. (Sometimes you'll get them even if you don't ask.) Embrace them! Often these people will be on a path similar to yours and will teach you something about your journey as you go along. Sometimes they might be on a very different path that's so unappealing that it affirms the direction you're going. Then, when life sends *you* people to be a mentor to, pay it forward.

4. Another important principle is to **accept that *angels are real*.** (You're currently reading a book about magic and becoming your own Genie, so I figure you can handle this bit about the angels without too much of a struggle.) Heaven is always trying to help you through any challenge or in the manifesting of any dream you have. Think of angels as being sort of the Genies of Heaven—always trying to help make your wishes come true! However, angels honor your God-given free will. So if you want their help, you have to ask them—just like you would a Genie! Create a relationship with your angels and your life will improve in ways you can't imagine.

5. Our next principle is simple: **Have faith**. Believe. Having a strong and powerful faith that the Universe loves you is one of the best things you can ever do for yourself. We're going back to the metaphorical gym here, but faith is a muscle you build up. It's literally like developing a strong heart. Faith is a magnet for joy. Joy is a magnet for magic.

I don't mean to steal a line from any amazing spiritual divas here, but as author and publisher Louise Hay always said, "Life loves you." It just does. In life, things will happen that will bring you great happiness and laughter. Life will also bring you sadness and tears. Both are powerful guides leading you toward the highest joy possible. The happy stuff is easy to see right away. The not-so-happy stuff takes more faith. So . . . have faith!

6. The last basic principle to having a fantastic relationship with your inner Genie is to **love yourself**. Love those around you.

Love your angels and say thank you to them. Thank the Universe that you're alive. Have a grateful heart, and the Divine will fill it with more happiness than you know what to do with. Which, of course, will make life all the more . . . magical!

$\mathcal{G}$ENIE $\mathcal{A}$CADEMY

Welcome to the Genie Academy! Throughout this book, you'll find lessons at the end of each chapter that will reinforce the concepts we've just gone over and show you real-life applications of the principles. You can do your Genie Academy lessons as you go along or save them all up to do after you've finished reading. In any case, please make the commitment to yourself to do them. They will help you turn the words on these pages into real magic in your life.

✦ ✦ ✦

Lesson #1: Negativity Check

You'll need either a voice recorder or a small notebook that will fit in your purse or pocket.

For the next two or three days, pay very close attention to your thoughts as well as the words you say out loud. Whenever you think or say something negative about yourself or those close to you, write it down or record it into your "negative thinking" journal or record.

Once you've completed this process, find a place where you can be quiet with your own thoughts without being interrupted. Take your pocket-size journal or voice recorder and copy or transcribe those thoughts onto the left side of a page in a fresh notebook. You'll likely be quite startled by the number of negative thoughts and words you introduced into your reality.

Now it's time to devise magical antidotes to what you've been creating that you really don't want in your life. Down the right side of the paper, you're going to write a corrective thought for each of these negative statements. Here's an example of what that might look like:

"I'm so clumsy."   "I'm graceful in all my movements."

"I'm not smart enough   "There's nothing I can't accomplish if I
to do that."   set my mind to it."

"Bob doesn't really care   "Bob loves me the best he can."
about me."

Once you have your negative-thinking antidotes, you're going to use them every time you say or think those negative statements. If you catch yourself saying, "I'm so clumsy," stop and say, "No, that's not correct; I'm graceful in all of my movements."

If necessary, keep your negative-thinking antidotes with you so that you can refer to them at any point when your thoughts or words don't match the reality you want to create.

* *

Getting Out of the Genie Lamp

Tales of Genies often begin with one who is stuck in a lamp or a bottle until someone comes along and releases them in exchange for wishes. However, *you* are your own Genie, so you'll have to get *yourself* out of that lamp to make your wishes come true!

So the Genie lamp, in our metaphor, refers to whatever is keeping you trapped or, at least, in the illusion of entrapment. In other words, it's the ways in which you might be blocking your own magic. The walls of your Genie lamp that keep you trapped are made up of three materials: *regret, self-blame or judgment*, and *unforgiveness*.

What's Holding You Back?

You've already taken the first step toward removing these blocks and getting yourself unstuck from where you've been. Simply by reading this book, you've made the choice to live a happier, more magical life where your dreams come true. Now, to keep the momentum going, you must let go of the past. When you focus on everything that's gone wrong and the ways in which your life hasn't measured up to your expectations, then it becomes difficult to have faith that things will change. If you spend all your time looking backward, then you'll never move forward.

Throughout your life, you'll also have moments of bliss— times of such utter joy that you'd love to live in them forever. But you can't live in the past. You might have some success re-creating moments that are similar, but after expressing gratitude for what has been, you must then move forward. Focus your Genie magic on creating totally new moments of happiness throughout your life. Never stop making new and exciting moments! You're an infinite supply of Divine manifesting energy.

The next thing that you'll have to do is to admit to your own drama. I know that most people say that they dislike drama and that they run from it as fast as they can. However, it's important that you sit down and really evaluate your relationship to drama. Oftentimes, the same people who say they hate drama are the ones who are devouring it like candy!

For example, pretend that you just got some news. I'm not talking about big, happy news like "We're getting married!" Maybe your car's engine is a goner, and now you're going to have to get a new car. Or perhaps you just heard bad news about someone else: "Did you know that Marie is leaving her husband?"

When unfortunate things are happening to you or others you know, and within minutes you're posting about it on social media and texting your friends to share the bad news, then you might be a *drama-holic*. If you run around telling the drama-filled, unfortunate stories that unfold in your life to everyone, the Universe is only going to give you *more* drama-filled, unfortunate stories to tell.

I think that some of the problems with our drama-holic society come from television and movies. Big drama-filled stories are what get people to tune in or go to the theater. Reality television is particularly guilty of skewing our perceptions of what makes a "normal life," making it easy to get attached to the idea that life is *supposed* to be dramatic.

And you know what? Life *is* dramatic! But it can be dramatic in the happiest of ways. For example, you can tell your friends and family that your dreams are coming true. Wouldn't that be wonderful drama?

Negative drama stories do nothing but bring you down and hold you back, keeping you in a drama-holic loop that isn't going to get you where you want to go. And the belief that you're trapped by your circumstances is just one more negative, drama-holic story. So let go of the negativity. It just inhibits your desire to leave the lamp.

FORGET THE REGRET

Let's start with the first trap of the Genie lamp: *regret*, a completely useless emotion. It makes sure that your gaze is firmly in the rearview mirror, focused on the past. Think about that analogy for a moment: Imagine if you were to try to drive your car solely while looking in the rearview mirror. What would happen? I suspect you'd be driving in fear the entire time. You wouldn't successfully get where you wanted to go because your trip would probably end in a terrible wreck.

When you regret something you've lost, like a relationship, you may not be able to start new relationships or enjoy the ones you do find in the here and now. Focusing on your regret may also cause you to continually kick yourself for something you did that you've judged as "bad." Even if you have truly done something unfortunate, you might be judging yourself unfairly.

Either way, by living in the regret of that event, you diminish your own self-worth. Your low self-confidence keeps you from believing that you deserve a happy life. Focusing on regret can also create unending fear that you'll make further mistakes.

I will allow that regret has *one* redeeming moment. And when I say "moment," I really mean that. Regret can provide you with the insight that your behavior, or your choices, has not been up to the standards you have set for your life. And in that *moment* of epiphany, you can learn. You can become determined not to repeat that mistake or error in judgment in the future. But that should last only as long as it takes for you to ask forgiveness from anyone who was harmed and then—and this is probably the most important part—to forgive yourself.

My mom was both mother and father to me and taught me many things that have helped me to have what I consider to be a very magical life. Her one little quirk, though, wasn't that she lived in regret, but in the *fear* of regret.

She would be so scared that she'd make a choice she'd regret that she couldn't make a choice at all. Helping her buy a new car was beyond challenging. Since I lived across the country from my mom, I have my dear brother-in-law, Ted, to thank for many of those car-shopping expeditions. Ted was infinitely patient with her, as it always took an extensive amount of searching and the need to drive a particular car many times. And when we were building her a new house, well . . . oy.

What I learned from my mom in that regard was that a fear of regret can be just as debilitating as regret itself.

A fear of regret shows up in a lot of the intuitive readings that I do for people. They write to me and ask things like: "Did I somehow miss meeting my soul mate?" or, "Should I have taken that career opportunity? Did I lose out on my chance to follow my life purpose?"

These types of questions break my heart. I have a great deal of compassion for people who are living in regret or fear that they have somehow messed up their lives in a way that can't be repaired.

As a strong believer in a loving and benevolent Universe, I don't actually believe it's possible to somehow permanently ruin something beautiful that's supposed to happen in your life. And so when I get those questions, my heart goes out to the questioner. And then I do everything I can to assure them that nothing is lost . . . nothing is ruined . . . everything will be fine. There's a reason you didn't marry that childhood sweetheart. It's probably because there's someone way better for you. But if you're looking backward and living in regret, you're not going to see Mr. (or Ms.) Right when he (or she) is standing right in front of you.

Regret and fear are intertwined. One leads to the other. As I said, if you live your life in regret, then you come to fear your own ability to make choices. You may wish for positive things in your life, but you have no confidence that they'll come to you or even that you deserve them.

You become trapped in the Genie lamp.

The cure for regret is forgiveness of self and others, as well as the faith that the best is still yet to come. Release regret and you're one-third of the way out of the lamp.

HERE COMES THE JUDGE(MENT)

Judgment and placing blame are the next hindrances to getting full control of your magic. Sadly, we're a judging society. We condemn others for their behavior without any idea of what their story is or what they have had to deal with in their lives. We blame whole groups of people for our problems and the challenges facing our planet. We harshly judge *ourselves* for our lack of success or our failed relationships.

The reason why judging others is a trap is that in doing so, we anticipate that others are almost certainly judging us. No one wants to be judged, yet everyone seems to be doing it. It's like a never-ending ride on a carousel, going nowhere.

Get off the carousel. Stop judging people. Keep your focus on your own contributions to the world. If others are doing things that you find are outside your own personal moral code, then get involved in a positive and proactive way that matches your Divine guidance. But leave the judging part out of it.

Perhaps even more importantly, show some compassion for yourself. You're human. You may occasionally take actions you aren't proud of. But instead of beating yourself up, realize that at any given moment you're always doing the best you can. Each bump in the road teaches you to take a different route the next time. Instead of berating yourself, pat yourself on the back for having learned something that will make you a better person who makes better choices in the future.

Wow! Look at you! You're two-thirds of the way out of that lamp!

ForGiftNess

The last thing keeping you in that lamp is unforgiveness—both of others and yourself. There's an old saying that might be a bit clichéd, but it's still very relevant. It has many variations, but the one I like to use is: "Holding on to unforgiveness is like drinking poison and expecting the other person to die."

Refusing to let go of anger, resentment, or even guilt about something you or someone else did in the past is completely toxic. If the unforgiveness is toward another person, you might feel that you're punishing them for whatever they did to you. But I assure you, the person truly being punished is you. You're the one feeling the greatest pain. The other person may desperately want your forgiveness, but if they don't get it, eventually they'll give up and let it go. They'll move on. But you'll still be suffering in that toxic energy, rehashing over and over what was done to you.

Unforgiveness keeps you permanently connected energetically to the other person and their painful behavior toward you. Why would you ever want that?

There's a common misunderstanding about forgiveness that I used to see in my private practice of doing psychic readings. Many people would misconstrue forgiving the other person as saying that what they did was "okay." Nothing could be further from the truth. You can forgive someone, thereby freeing yourself from further torture, without ever agreeing that their behavior was in any way acceptable. By forgiving someone, you're not validating their actions.

Forgiving someone is not a "gift" or free pass you're giving them. It's a gift you're giving *yourself*.

Another curious but not uncommon feeling expressed by my clients was that if they forgave the other person, they were somehow allowing for the possibility that the hurtful experience might happen again. Forgiving someone doesn't erase what you've learned. It doesn't diminish your ability to protect yourself. You can have your eyes wide open and still have your heart free of the pain of the past.

Self-forgiveness is just as critical as forgiving someone else. Of all the barriers to getting out of the Genie lamp, this one is probably the most significant, because a lack of self-forgiveness is like regret, judgment, blaming, and unforgiveness all rolled up in one big bundle, stopping up the lamp and keeping you locked inside. The statement "I'll never forgive myself" is like stuffing a cork into the lamp, blocking your way to a magical life. Forgiving yourself is a magical *gift* that only *you* can give yourself.

Here's a news flash for you: *God isn't keeping tabs.* Regardless of what you may have been taught, God is only loving you along the journey, all the while thinking about how adorable you are. He's hoping that you'll soon figure out for yourself just how radiantly beautiful and magical you are, and thinking just how awesome a day that will be.

So if you're having trouble forgiving yourself, consider this: Heaven forgives you. Your angels forgive you. God forgives you. And if you have all that forgiveness shining down upon you, you must be pretty darned forgivable!

So get with the program. Whatever it was, it's over now. You're a better person. You have amazing things to contribute to the world, and your magical life awaits!

Congratulations! You're out of the lamp!

* *

$\mathcal{G}$ENIE $\mathcal{A}$CADEMY

Lesson #2: Drama-holic Pulse Check

Just like in Lesson #1, you'll need a small pad of paper that will fit in your purse or pocket or a voice recorder. What you're going to be doing is taking note of every time you participate in a bit of drama. This includes items such as:

- *Sharing* distressing or dramatic stories about your life with others

- Being a welcome participant in *hearing* stories or gossip about others

- *Posting* intense stories on social-media platforms

- Actively *engaging* in situations requiring you to be in conflict with others, which could have been avoided

- Spending time telling and *retelling* stories in your mind about how you should have handled or will handle an issue with another person

- *Anything* that gets your anxiety level moving toward the ceiling

If the list has more than two or three things on it by the end of the day, you *may* be a drama-holic. If so, it's time to purge that behavior. Look for common things that trigger your attraction to drama. Is it always the same people you're interacting with at the time? Does it make you feel important when you have the "scoop" on a story before anyone else? If you're a drama-holic, then it's time to face that truth so that you can start avoiding the people or situations that pull you into that loop of anxious or negative behavior.

✦ ✦ ✦

Lesson #3: Releasing Regret

If regret is a big part of your life, then I'd like to help you let that go. So let's start by making a list of anything that's keeping you looking backward instead of forward.

Find a quiet place where you won't be disturbed and take a few breaths. Try to bring yourself to a peaceful place. Now think backward. Are there any situations from the past that you think of often with regret? Most often the most troubling situations will cross your mind on a regular basis even if it's been a long time since the event occurred. Write them down.

If you come across small things that you don't think of very often, it's all right to jot those down, as well. These may be things you did in childhood or your youth that you almost never think of, but that you wish had never happened or had had a different outcome. If we're going to release regret, let's get rid of all of it!

Once you have your list, I want you to write down what you learned from each situation. Look for something positive. It might be that it made you a better person going forward. Perhaps it showed you the value of friendships or love in your life. Maybe you now know a great deal more about who you are and what you want from life. Do your best to find *something* that came from that moment you're regretting that's positive and write it down.

Once you have the list of your regrets and the positive things that came from those situations, you're going to say a prayer or meditation of forgiveness and release for yourself. It can be whatever words come to you, but an example of that might be:

Dear Divine source of love,

Please help me to release these feelings of regret. I ask that I receive the forgiveness of all that are involved as well as forgiveness of self at this time of release. Create for me the peace of letting go of "all that was" so that I might embrace the "now," knowing that these experiences have made me a more compassionate and kind person. Help me to remember at all times that your love is propelling me toward joy, toward fulfillment, and toward my dreams come true. I now release all feelings of guilt, regret, and sadness in favor of the peace of forgiveness and the remembering of how loved I am.
And so it is.

Once you've done that, you're going to release the paper you wrote your regrets and lessons on. I prefer to burn it. Make sure that you do so safely, ensuring the fire will be easily contained and can't spread past the paper you're releasing. If that isn't possible, then you can simply scrunch it up into a ball and toss it into the trash while taking deep breaths. Keep in mind that you are throwing away the last of your regret.

* *

— CHAPTER 3 —

What Wishes Will You Grant Yourself?

"Star light, star bright. First star I see tonight. I wish I may . . . I wish I might . . . have the wish I wish tonight."

The question is: *What are you wishing for?* You see, everything you think can turn into a wish. You're constantly creating. Constantly crafting your present and your future. And so carrying emotions and attitudes with you each day is akin to making wishes. Fortunately, wishes often take a little while to manifest, so you have time to "unwish" what you thought about that guy who just cut you off in traffic.

When most people "make a wish" by blowing out the candles on a birthday cake or blowing away the seeds from a dandelion, they have a tendency to ask for something that they don't even believe can be theirs. They either don't see how to change their current circumstances or don't believe they're deserving of their dreams.

You can wish for whatever you like, but if you don't believe, then you're really just wishing for the opposite of what you want. What you *truly* believe to be likelier to happen will override your stated wish. If you *don't* believe it's possible, then you're just asking the Universe to match your expectations by keeping things the way they are.

CHOOSE A BETTER REALITY

A sense of unworthiness is running rampant through the world these days. And, of course, those who feel that they don't merit happiness are usually the people *most* deserving of it. At least that's how I've observed it. I travel around the world teaching, and I constantly see angelic people. Those sweet, kind folks who are constantly doing for others . . . always giving, rarely receiving, because they don't believe that they're good enough.

Wishing is a practice of **faith**. (That word is in boldface because it should be thought of as a bold endeavor!) Wishing requires you to claim that this is *your* moment. This is *your* time to shine and to be happy and to have what you want! But to do that, you must wish with optimism and confidence of your own deservingness.

You must make a wish of love that's turned inward.

No matter who you are or what your circumstances are, I want you to hear me now: You. Are. Deserving! You are, you are, you *are*. You deserve every dream you ever had. There's a reason you have those dreams, even if it was just to show you it wasn't what you wanted after all and to lead you to a new and better dream. All your dreams are real and important and valid. They're just waiting for you to open your arms and embrace them with happiness.

The great spiritual writer Esther Hicks once said, "Never face reality unless your reality is just the way you want it to be." Becoming your own Genie means having control over your reality. It's a bit like hitting the reset button on your life. You get in touch with your Genie and exit the lamp, and suddenly the world is one big magic bubble of potential. You have the opportunity to completely reinvent yourself. You're not just your own Genie; suddenly you're your own life designer!

For all this to happen, you'll have to make choices. You'll have to say yes to the person you want to create. You'll probably have to change, and I know that change can be frightening to people. Yet it can also be uplifting. Exhilarating! Making the right choices can take your life from *humdrum* to *fantastic* very quickly.

Choosing is a very important part of having a magical life. Its power can't be overstated. Truth be told, many people don't make a lot of powerful decisions in their lives. They may choose their careers, their homes, or their cars. People think that they decide whom to marry, where in the world to live, and whether to have children. But if they were truly honest with themselves and took the time to review these decisions very closely, a lot of them might find that they just went with the path of least resistance. They did what their parents, spiritual leaders, politicians, and friends expected them to do. They may live close to where they were born, have taken whatever jobs fell into their laps, and have married whoever happened to present themselves. They may have even told themselves that the person they married was the best they could do.

But, you see, this is not deciding . . . it's basically just coasting. This is abdicating responsibility for the direction your life will go. It can be tantamount to tossing all prospects for true joy in your life up into the air and hoping that the wind is blowing in the right direction to get you there.

Remember, you're a *Genie!* You don't have to just "hope" everything works out. You have magic, and through your conscious choices, you can make wishes come true!

"Oops! I Forgot My Life Purpose"

A few years ago, I was feeling pretty stuck, working for the government as a certified public accountant. I had already quit that life once back in 2001 but returned to it in 2005 when my fears got the best of me. I didn't know what I wanted to do with myself, but I knew I couldn't stay in accounting forever—especially not the job I was in.

I had lots of friends who did intuitive readings, but I wanted one from someone who didn't know me. I came across one person who had written a book, and something just sort of felt right about her. So I called her and scheduled a reading.

When we started the session, I told her that my main concern was that I didn't know what I wanted to do with my life.

She immediately replied, "Yes, you do."

I understood why she might say that, but I just very nicely corrected her. She came back at me pretty aggressively, saying that my angels were telling her that I knew exactly what I was supposed to be doing with my life.

We went back and forth about it a few times, and then I got irritated with her. I ended the session after just 20 minutes, even though I had paid for an hour.

Sometimes the right thing to do is to ignore the messenger but keep the message. I didn't like the way she delivered the message, but within three years I knew that she had been absolutely right. I had fully known when talking to her exactly what I wanted to do with my life. The problem was that I just didn't think it could happen!

I had already tried to do metaphysical work as my career for the previous four years and had gotten nowhere. My ego was taking this handy-dandy example and using that "failure" to limit my progress. Since I didn't believe that it was possible for me to do what I so yearned to do, I was left confused about my direction and purpose.

You have your dreams for a reason. You honestly do. Perhaps you're in a situation like I was in where you've "forgotten" your dreams because you've given up on them as even being possible. Well, it's time to remember those dreams, dust them off, and give them another look. Maybe your desires have changed, so those old dreams are no longer applicable. When I was a kid, I wanted to be an astronaut and travel among the stars in a beautiful spaceship, but that's not a dream that's relevant for me anymore.

On the other hand, the dream of becoming a spiritual teacher and author . . . now *that* put the stars back in my eyes. I just had to *remember* that it was my dream and then *believe* it was possible.

One of the things I highly recommend you do in order to get really clear on your wishes for your life is to examine your beliefs and let go of the ones that no longer work for you, hold you back, or make you feel bad or guilty. Basically, if a belief system keeps you from being your fullest, truest self, it needs to get the old heave-ho—tossed overboard from your little boat of life. Limiting beliefs about yourself and your ability to have whatever you want should also be jettisoned, pronto!

My friend Polly once told me that sometimes the dreams that come true are the ones you never even knew you had. I *love* that, because it's absolutely true! I know that in my life I can think back to magical and amazing things that happened to me that were just that: dreams that came true that I didn't even know about. In retrospect, those have absolutely been some of the very best "dreams come true" of my life.

WILLY-NILLY WISHING

Making wishes does take focus, though. I highly recommend that you fully understand what you're wishing for before asking Heaven and your angels. Not doing so is what I call "willy-nilly wishing." This falls under the category of: "Be careful what you wish for, as you just might get it."

In that same vein, I don't particularly subscribe to the idea that wishes must be kept secret. Sometimes I will talk with friends or family about what I'm wishing for. The clarity you gain can be incredibly freeing, especially if an insightful conversation suddenly causes you to realize: "Um . . . you know what? Maybe I don't want that after all!"

No matter how well I've thought a wish through—which I do, *sometimes*—it may not be the best thing for me. When that is the case, God will always give me something better. I have lots of friends who end their prayers with, "This I ask for, or something better." We should abide by that same sentiment when we make a wish.

Finally, it's important to dream *big*! You may have to break your wish down into manageable pieces—smaller wishes that lead to one big dream come true. But the long-term goal for yourself should be something amazing—something worthy of a big-time, child-of-the-Divine, magical Genie like you!

$\mathcal{G}$ENIE $\mathcal{A}$CADEMY

Lesson #4: Perfect-Life Bio

So here's a fun way to get some clarity on what wishes you might want to make come true for yourself. Find yourself a little quiet time. You don't have to have a lot, maybe 20 minutes. Grab a pen and paper, or a laptop . . . whatever way you like to write.

Now write your own biography as if your life was perfect—the way you would like it to be. Include every area, both in your professional and personal lives. That might look like: "Linda lives in her dream home in the suburbs of Seattle, Washington, with her husband, Allan. They have two wonderful children, Zack and Brianna. When she's not writing a book or running her animal rescue, her hobbies include salsa dancing . . ."

Now once you've done that, sit back and compare your dream bio to your current life. No fair beating yourself up if they don't match up very well. Remember, you're not grading or judging yourself. That's not the point. The point here is to see if you're headed in the direction of your dreams. Are your days, weeks, and months leading you on the path you want to be on? Are you taking at least baby steps toward the life you want to live?

If so, then bravo! You may still see areas in your bio that need more attention so that you can make adjustments to your path.

If your daily life is *not* leading you in the direction of your dream bio, then you've got some changes to make.

Look again at your Perfect-Life Bio. Which items in your description make you the most excited? What are you hoping for most? Focus on one particular item initially. Then consider whether making it come true feels to you like it's completely doable or a stretch. If it's a stretch, then break it down into smaller wishes and turn to those first.

— Chapter 4 —

Making the Magic Happen

Okay, let's review. You've learned some exciting and very empowering things about yourself and the Universe. You know there's magic weaving in and out of you and everything you see, that magic comes from God/Source/the Divine/choose-your-favorite-term, and *you* are a part of that magic! You realized your inner Genie is the part of you that can connect with that magic and manifest the life you want to live. You've learned the steps that get you out of that magic lamp so that you're free to make magic! Hopefully, you've even gotten clarity on what wishes you're ready to make come true for yourself (or you're working on that, at least).

Now the time has come to start learning about *how* to use your magic!

Heaven Is *So* Chatty!

I mentioned earlier that I attempted to follow the path of a spiritually based career for four years without success. But when I tried again a few years later, suddenly it all worked!

Would you like to know what I did differently?

(I *thought* you might.) Well, I started following my personal Divine guidance.

The Universe is *always* talking to us. The voices of angels, spiritual guides, and even the Divine itself never stop lovingly whispering how you might have greater joy in your life. The problem is that those precious whispers often get drowned out by this noisy world. You may forget to listen for them or be so convinced that they aren't there that you don't even bother to *try* to hear what they're saying.

Those messages are your Divine guidance. It's like the transmissions of your Divine Guidance Communication System (DGCS) are on a radio frequency that resonates in concert with that magical music inside you. These messages are always trying to help you to manifest the life you're dreaming of. Once you learn how to recognize or "hear" those messages—and start to follow their direction—you will gain more and more access to the magic within you.

So what does that look like—following one's Divine guidance? Well, in my own life, it went something like this . . .

For the past few years, I'd been getting the message that I should convert to vegetarianism. I'd learned that whenever a thought gets stuck in your head, you should pay attention to it, and this thought was definitely stuck in my head. In talking to my guardian angel Joshua about it, the conversation was similar to this:

Joshua: Radleigh.
Radleigh: Yes, Josh?
Joshua: You're a vegetarian.
Radleigh: What? Oh no, I'm not!
Joshua: Yes. Yes, you are.
Radleigh: <in a whiny voice> But! But what about *cheeseburgers*?
Joshua: Trust me on this one. You're a vegetarian.
Radleigh: <heavy sigh> Okay. Fine. I'm a vegetarian.

A few weeks later, this exchange happened:

Joshua: Radleigh.
Radleigh: <somewhat leery> What?
Joshua: You're sober.
Radleigh: Oh, the heck I am!
Joshua: <laughing> No, really. You are!
Radleigh: But! But what about *martinis*?
Joshua: You're sober.
Radleigh: <trying not to cry> Okay. Fine. I'm sober.

And then this happened:

Joshua: Radleigh.
Radleigh:<fingers in ears> LALALALALALALALA! I can't hear you!
Joshua: Yes, you can. That little trick only works on the ego.
Radleigh: Okay, fine. What now?
Joshua: No more caffeine.
Radleigh: <silence>
Joshua: Radleigh?
Radleigh: Okay. Fine. I'm not even going to argue about it. No more caffeine.
Joshua: Good job.

Since I had those conversations and followed my guidance, I completely left the accounting world. I have signed over 20 contracts with my publisher and spoken at over 70 events in 10 countries. In short, suddenly the magic was flowing like a Smoky Mountain river.

You might be thinking, *Well, gee, Radleigh, not everyone can hear their angels like you.* Actually, you'd be wrong about that. I'll give you the inside scoop on chatting up the great winged wonders in the next chapter.

In the meantime, it's important to realize that the angels, Heaven, and God aren't trying to be stubborn or difficult when they ask you to make certain changes. What they're trying to do is make you an energetic match for the life you want to live.

Your own guidance does not necessarily involve vegetarianism, or sobriety, or a decaffeinated life. Don't follow my Divine guidance; follow *yours*. Whatever that might be, take action.

You know what you're being called to do. It's a nagging feeling or group of thoughts that starts with *I really should be* _____. The blank will be filled with positive actions, not negative, ego-based ones. Things that you *know* are good for you and would improve your life. Even as you read this, you're undoubtedly thinking, *Oh yeah. I know some of the things that I'm being guided to do.*

Because this is such an important concept, let me give you another way to think about it. You've heard the saying, "Like attracts like," yes? Everything in the Universe is made up of energy and is attracted to energy on the same wavelength. Your thoughts and actions will attract to you more of what you focus on.

Let's pretend that your dream is to become a doctor. And let's say that being a doctor works best when the energy around you is emerald green. However, your energy is currently pale blue. (You'll recall that colors simply represent different *wavelengths* of light.) While there's nothing wrong with pale blue—it's a perfectly lovely color—it's just not the *best* energy for being a doctor. As soon as you let the Universe know that your wish is to become a doctor, it starts to chitchat away at you like a neighbor with absolutely nothing better to do. Seriously! The Universe just won't shut up until you start to listen to the guidance it has for you on how to turn your pale blue energy into the emerald green necessary to successfully manifest becoming a doctor. But you have to listen!

You may already know a lot about what your Divine guidance is trying to tell you. Perhaps you've been getting messages such as *Take up yoga* or *It's time to let go of caffeine.* If so, I highly recommend that you begin to follow that guidance right away.

Even if you're already aware of some of the changes you're being called to make, I still suggest that you partake in the Genie Academy lesson at the end of this chapter for two reasons:

- **First**, you may have come to realize from Lesson #4: Perfect-Life Bio that you have some wishes you want to come true that you weren't aware of. That means that the Universe might start sending you new guidance to make sure you're an energetic match for your dreams.

- **Second**, the ego loves to drown out Divine guidance, so the lesson may help you discover important pieces that are hidden from you.

The Faith Gym

Once you've learned to tune in to your DGCS, you have to *act* upon that guidance. If you find yourself making excuses, then stop and ask yourself why: *Why would I want to delay my perfect life? Why not start today?* The answer is probably that your ego is playing games with your mind.

Magic is pretty amazing stuff, but it usually requires action on your part. Not *everything* requires Divine guidance and changes to your life in order to become manifest, but more often than not, the *big* things do.

I know, I know . . . you were hoping you could just cross your arms and blink and then stuff would happen. Well, you may be pleased to know that sometimes that really is the case!

However, if you were to analyze what was *really* going on when something seemed to manifest right out of thin air, you would probably discover that you had actually wished for it without realizing it. There were no negative thoughts you'd attached to the wish. You'd released it to God without any sense that you didn't deserve it. Then—*voilà!*—it showed up.

If you have a hard time feeling that you deserve your wishes, I want you to do the following:

Make a list of every wonderful thing you ever did for the world or someone else. Now is not the time for humility! Write down each and every nice act you can remember. If you're truly honest with yourself, you'll be astonished by how long this list will be. This is proof positive of how worthy you are and that you deserve your wishes, big and small!

Let's say that you've gotten Divine guidance and are following through on that advice. You're ready to take action, but frankly you have really big dreams. Your faith is a little shaky, and you have no idea where to start. The answer to that dilemma is to take actions that are the same size as your faith. Remember, building faith is like building muscles. You start small and work your way up.

Let's say your dream is to accumulate $1 million. Do you have absolute, unshakable faith that that will happen? Because if you do, it's on the way! But if there's even a bit of nagging doubt in your mind, then that million dollars is probably locked up tight in your Genie lamp.

So let's see how big your faith is.

Do you believe that you could just suddenly receive $1,000 in the coming week? No? Okay, what about $100? $50? $10? Oh, come on! You can find $10 in a purse you thought you'd completely emptied or under the seat of your car. So can we agree on $10? Good!

Begin your wishing work by asking for $10, then *stay awake*. Notice what is happening in your life, and especially notice what happens as it relates to the manifesting of your wishes.

Before you start digging around in the cushions of your couch, let's get clear on the nature of abundance. Yes, if you found a $10 bill on the floor, it would be a clear manifestation of your wish that you could easily recognize. But what if your co-worker unexpectedly picked up your $10 tab at lunch—wouldn't that count as fulfilling your wish? If a friend of yours gifted you a box of chocolates because she was on a diet, then that would count, too! In any case, you started by wishing for the magical, energetic worth of $10, and you got it. Excellent! Your faith got just a little bit stronger.

How do you feel about wishing for $20 now? Think you can do it? If so, go for it! If not, then go another week wishing for the $10, until you do feel good about being able to manifest the $20.

You can repeat this exercise on any of your wishes. If you have big dreams—and you should!—then you may need to grow your faith by building it up incrementally until it has reached the level of your big dream. The small pieces will always lead to greater accomplishments, and soon you'll be on your way!

GENIE-OLOGY

In order to have your magical life, you need to *believe*, somewhere down deep, that you're amazing. You have to *know* that your life has beautiful meaning. You have to *have faith* that when your day comes around to pass through the gates of Heaven, you're going to arrive to a rousing burst of applause. Having that kind of belief in yourself puts a restraining order on your doubting, negative ego. If your mind, heart, and soul are in on the task, then your ego is vastly outnumbered. It doesn't stand a chance.

One powerful way to help build this level of self-esteem and make magic happen is to get fellow Genies in on the action. This requires seeking out others who share your beliefs and your desire to have a magical life. It's kind of like having the same magical DNA, so I call that *Genie-ology*!

While large organizations have their place, I'm a big believer in the power of small groups. To really create your dreams, it works best when you have an intimate group where everyone is crystal clear on the big picture and the details of what everyone is wanting to create.

You may need to have different groups for the different wishes you're manifesting. For example, in one of my groups, I have three guys who have been in my life for almost two decades. We're the "bestest of besties." To us, we're truly brothers and behave as such. I can turn to them for anything, and they're there to cheer me on! For the most part, we support each other with personal life goals. Frankly, just having them in my life *is* the fulfillment of a personal life goal, and I consider it one of my most successful Genie wishes come true.

I also have another group, consisting of three women whom I call my "Superhero friends"! We make sure we're on target with our career goals, check each other on our crap, and pray for one another. Sometimes the lines are a little blurred, and we talk about personal things in my "career goals" group, but that's perfectly okay. There don't need to be strong boundaries and hard-and-fast rules about allowed topics. Just let the support and conversation unfold organically.

A small support group instills in you a sense of empowerment and of your own value. Everyone needs a cheerleader in life, and there's no reason why you can't build your own cheerleading squad! Gather a few close friends, and make sure to have regular calls or get-togethers. There's no need to take yourselves too seriously—laugh, drink tea, and form goals. Be there for each other on good days and bad days. Remember that support is a two-way street, and giving is just as important as receiving. So if your phone rings or you get an SOS text, you do have to respond!

Then again, perhaps your goals aren't necessarily something you want to share with your friends or immediate acquaintances. I know what it's like to have good friends but not feel that I can talk to them about what I'm fascinated by or concerned about at the moment. In my hometown, the topics I was drawn to were not exactly considered mainstream. There was just no one to talk to about angels or tarot cards or any of the myriad things that made me different. And so I turned to the Internet. I found people who lived in four or five other states who shared my interests and passions. With the countless opportunities for connection that exist through social media, there's no reason you can't put together your own Genie-ology team.

BLESSED/STRESSED/YES/MESS!

You will have to be patient at first as you wait for your wishes to come true. You're a newbie playing with your magic. Some dreams require things to change not only in *your* life but also in the lives of others. The gears of your Genie magic may at first turn a little slowly, but things will start to speed up as you work more and more with your spiritual gifts and Heaven has time to reorganize earthly situations to match your new desires.

Eventually, you're going to start to notice that the things you want begin to manifest faster and faster and with bigger and bigger results. This brings us to a concept I call "Blessed/Stressed/Yes/Mess!"

During the time I was writing this book, I had a lot going on. I had two books to write, an angel oracle card deck to create, an app I was working on, an extensive video course to film, a three-day live course to plan, and a European tour coming up. Oh, *and* I also got married and promised my new husband that we'd somehow squeeze a honeymoon into the same period. This was all on top of my regular activities of hosting a radio show and social-media video show, as well as providing daily support to the thousands of students of a video course already in place.

In short, I don't think I had ever been so *blessed* in my entire life! There wasn't a single thing on my list that I wasn't elated to be doing. All of it was a part of my magical life.

I'm also not sure if I'd ever been so *stressed* in my entire life! Now mind you, this was all "good stress" from so many wishes coming true at once. I had no desire to give up even one of the many things I was working on.

The problem was that I continued to agree to everything I was offered. Radio interviews, magazine articles—you name it, and I just said *yes*. And you know what that turned into?

A *mess*.

I believe that *yes* is a very magical word, but that period of my life taught me just how magical *no* could be. *Blessed* had turned to *stressed* so that each new *yes* made my life a *mess*.

Once you're in touch with your magic, your inner Genie might just start granting wishes right and left! The magic spirals upward and out in the world, and it can get a little out of control. So if you're going to be your own Genie, you have to stay *in control* of your magic. Having a magical life is all about joy, not anxiety.

I wholeheartedly agree with the common phrase, "Say yes to life!" But when life starts to become too much, it's okay—and healthy—to say no (or even "wait") while you bring one wish to life before taking on any others.

Happy Magic

Up until now, we've spent a lot of time on the intellectual side of using your magic. Magic, however, is also a very emotional thing. Having your head in the right space is crucial for manifesting a magical life, but if your emotions are fighting your thoughts, you're not going to get very far.

One of the awesome things about using your emotions in your magical life is that they don't actually have to be centered on what you're trying to manifest. While this might seem odd to you, it's actually great if you're having trouble keeping faith or remaining optimistic about creating your big, beautiful new life. Perhaps you're managing to keep your thoughts positive about making your wishes come true, but deep inside you have nagging doubts or a sense of pessimism. Well, you need to get in touch with your feelings of happiness and elation—even if those emotions have absolutely nothing to do with your wishes.

You see, the Universe is a very magical and joyful place! That's just the vibe it resonates to. So when you're in a place of delight or exuberance, you're vibrating *with* the Universe instead of *against* it. Like attracts like, remember?

It shouldn't be a surprise that you magically create happier outcomes with joy than with worry or fear. It's similar to the saying, "You attract more bees with honey than with vinegar." So if you can keep your thoughts in check while walking around feeling happy, you've got some serious magic happening.

It doesn't matter where your joyful emotions and memories come from. Just discover your "happy place" and practice being able to bring those emotions to the surface whenever you need them.

Let me give you an example from my own life . . .

I really don't like to talk too much about my age. First of all, I don't feel that my energy matches the number of candles on my birthday cake (assuming I even allowed *anyone* to put candles on my birthday cake). Focusing on how "old" I am just manifests feeling old, so why do that?

However, in this case I'll just come right out and tell you that I'm five years old. Yes, *five*. At least, on the inside I am! I may look like a grown-up guy, but at heart I'm a total kid. And nothing brings out my inner child more than the holidays.

Christmas trees and menorah candles. Yule logs and hot cocoa. Snowmen, dreidels, candy canes, shiny packages, reindeer, and jolly old elves all dressed in red and green. Just seeing that list, it's all I can do to contain myself and keep from jumping up and down and squealing!

I think the biggest thing for me is the strings of lights. I just *love* the lights. As for our house, we go old-school here. Remember those big bulbs? They're called C9s, and the colors are white, orange, green, red, and blue in that *exact* order. (Sorry, but the order is important!) Every year, people try to talk me out of those old-style bulbs and get me to go all LED and stuff . . . but, nope, I'm not doing it! Those lights, and the lights on the tree, are what really get my inner child going!

Whenever I'm aware that I'm feeling worried or anxious about something, I realize that I'm shutting down my magic. And I don't like that. So I take a minute and close my eyes and think about those holiday lights. I might even put on the appropriate music. (Yes, I'm one of those "holiday music in July" people; don't judge.) I let those giddy emotions take over, and suddenly I'm happy! I'm in joy! I remember that the Universe wants me to feel this way all the time, and I hold on to those feelings.

It's obvious that my happy place is the holidays, but yours will likely be something else. Whatever it is, once you are able to bring up those emotions, focus on your dream while keeping in mind those optimistic feelings. Remind yourself that you deserve all the happiness in the world—that it's coming to you because you're a worthy and magical child of God.

Now, you might have a hard time keeping those joyous emotions going while you're thinking about your dreams. If contemplating your desires brings you down, then *don't do it*! Just go back to your happy place.

KEEPING FAITH IN THE MAGIC

It's time to talk about the aspects of being your own Genie that can be a little more challenging. You're going to need an unwavering, solid, *stubborn* belief that everything—absolutely *everything*—that happens to you is meant to eventually bring you joy in some way. I'm sorry to start boldfacing words again, but this isn't faith, it's **faith**. It's a belief in a God that's always loving you, eternally trying to help you, and never stops adoring you.

This is a philosophy that I hold in my heart completely and absolutely without any doubt. Bad things, or things that we label "bad," happen in everyone's life. I'm no exception. While I've got my own little scary list of experiences, I can explain how almost every one of them is a part of the happiness I enjoy today. The few that I can't explain, I have utter **faith** that in time I *will* be able to explain them. While it's great to have a nice little "answer hook" to hang your faith upon for every little challenging thing that occurred in your life, it's not necessary. **faith** doesn't require answers. (That's why it's **faith**.)

Like most everyone, I've had to endure the loss of people and animals I love. Time has healed the pain of some of those losses, while others continue to bring tears. From them, I learned the importance of every single moment. I came to see the need to infuse magic not just into the special times but into every moment. My **faith** that those passed-over loved ones are in Heaven and that they watch out for me has been born out through signs and miracles that had their fingerprints (or paw prints) all over them.

Physical and emotional abuse as a child taught me compassion and kindness for others. It also brought me the realization that I can never know the reasons why someone might be bitter, unfriendly, or guarded, because I don't know what they have lived through.

An unbelievably cruel romantic relationship in my youth taught me the true value of later relationships that were tender, loving, supportive, and profound. It also taught me something about my own value and self-worth so that I never let anyone ever treat me so horribly again.

We can greatly dislike or even abhor experiences that occur in our lives. I'm certainly not debating that. But the ability to maintain the **faith** that something about every experience has the ability to make you stronger, more resilient, and a better person . . . well, my friend, *that* is a big part of the magic. And that **faith** will bring you more happiness in the long run than you could possibly imagine.

TRICKY MAGIC: LETTING GO

There's one last piece to making the magic happen that I want to share with you. Of all the things I've explained, this is the part I think most people have the biggest challenge with.

You have to let go.

You've figured out what you want to create. You've visualized it. You've got your head and your heart in sync, and you've even starting taking action. And . . . now I say to *let go*?

I know it sounds crazy . . . maybe even a little contradictory. However, just remember what I've told you from the beginning: *believing* is critical to getting that magical life you want. You have to trust that the Divine is the source of all magic. Nothing is beyond its ability to create.

The mistake that people make with their wishes is to try to tell God "how" and "when" they will come true. They cling to every detail with a sort of desperate energy that's anything *but* faith. In fact, it's fear. Fear won't manifest you a magical life, but it will definitely manifest you a very unhappy one.

Every single time that I ask the Universe for something and then let it go, it seems to manifest in my life in record speed! Although some wishes require action, others are completely out of your hands. There won't be any action you can take; you'll just have to wish and wait.

I've even made wishes and forgotten about them; then—*poof!*—they manifested. Those incidents always make me laugh. One of them occurred while I was writing this book . . .

My new husband, Lee, and I had chosen our favorite place to get away for our honeymoon, which also happens to be a spot where a certain celebrity is known to visit from time to time. While I admire this celebrity's work, he had absolutely nothing to do with the choice of our honeymoon destination. Still, I couldn't help but wonder, *What if we were to run into him?* It was a fun thought, but nothing I really put much energy into. Just a little wish I made and then let go of.

One morning, Lee and I were at the grocery store getting supplies, and—*poof!*—in walked that celebrity. I couldn't believe it. We didn't want to be intrusive, but we did get to say hello and let him know how much we love his work, and he responded to us very graciously.

Now let's break this down: What are the odds that a celebrity I respect and admire would walk into a grocery store at the same time we were there? (This wasn't a tiny town, either. We were right outside a major city where celebrities tend to live.) What are the odds that the celebrity would walk into the same *part* of the grocery store I was currently shopping in so that I would see him?

That, my friend, is the power of letting go!

When you try to control how the magic unfolds instead of just letting it come to you in the Divine's all-knowing way, it's basically putting your inner Genie back into the lamp. And, as I've already explained, the magic doesn't happen in the lamp. It happens *outside* the lamp.

* *

GENIE ACADEMY

Lesson #5: What Is Your Divine Guidance Telling You?

I suggest that you do this lesson over several days just so you can gain real clarity about discerning what is your Divine guidance as opposed to your ego just ganging up on you. Divine guidance feels like gentle, positive ideas that come into your mind. The ego feels more like berating outbursts or prolonged guilty feelings of not being good enough.

At the beginning of each day that you're working on this lesson, incorporate something like the following into your daily prayers or meditations. I'm using the word *God*, but you can substitute whatever word fits with your spiritual beliefs.

Dear God,

I am so very excited to be on this journey to make my dreams come true. I know that in order to be successful, I need to listen to and act upon any Divine guidance you're sending my way. Please make that guidance crystal clear to me. Let me know what I'm being asked to do through repetition of the message, signs, and the experience of positive emotions when I think about the changes being asked of me. I ask that you help make the changes flow easily and fill me with the necessary motivation to be successful.

Of course, feel free to adapt this prayer for guidance and support in any way you feel led to do. If the changes you feel you need to make create negative emotions within you, such as guilt or helplessness, then ask God to help you release those emotions and make you feel empowered instead.

If the negative feelings continue, then the proposed "changes" might be your ego distracting you from the changes you *really* need to make. Set those things aside for now and concentrate on the Divine guidance that feels good and attainable to you. If you're really meant to work on the things that don't feel good right now, they'll come back around later. Then you'll be stronger because of the progress you've already made, and thus better able to deal with them.

Some people do best making one change at a time. That was certainly the case for me. Over the days that you are asking for clarity on your Divine guidance, pay attention to the item that comes up the most. That is the one you'll want to start with.

✦ ✦ ✦

Lesson #6: Gifts of Joy

Write down what you want to manifest on a few pieces of paper. Write just *one* thing on each slip of paper, not a whole list. If you already have a list, that's cool. What a Genie you are! Just get more paper and transfer each item onto a fresh sheet.

Next, you're going to put each piece of paper in a separate box. These boxes can be small or large. It's up to you. I like a variety.

Now wrap each of these boxes as gifts (gifts to yourself from Heaven!) with as much joy as you can muster. Bring up your most euphoric memories from your happy place while you're wrapping these gifts from the Divine to sweet little magical *you*! As you cut and fold, ask the angels to help you make those dreams come true. Then put these magical gifts somewhere special where you can look at them when you want.

If you ever start to feel down or worried about your dreams, remember those wrapped gifts and smile. Stay in that joyful anticipatory state. Because that's exactly what any not-quite-yet-manifested dream of yours is: just an unopened gift! It's coming, but you're just going to have to wait a bit more.

Feel yourself getting in the vibe of the Universe, and watch magical things start to happen!

* *

CHAPTER 5

Your Magical Helpers

You're going to need help to uncover and begin your magical life. Heaven will send a mentor or teacher your way when you need one—whether you ask or not! I've been blessed throughout my life to have had several such teachers. In my first job as an accountant, I had an amazing mentor. What she taught me about accounting was greatly overshadowed by what she taught me about professionalism, maturity, and how you treat people. While I had other mentors in my accounting career, none ever had the impact on me that she did.

When I left accounting the first time, I started feeding the little bookworm inside me even more than I had in the past. Spiritual authors and lecturers grabbed my attention, and their teachings woke me up. I started to see the magical life I wanted; I realized that I wanted what *they* were living, the life of a spiritual teacher.

In 2003, someone suggested that I take the Angel Therapy Practitioner (ATP) course taught by Doreen Virtue. Curiously, as much as I was head over heels into angels, I had never heard of her, but I was instantly fascinated by her work. When I called to register for the ATP course, the person on the phone exclaimed, "Wow, you must really be meant to be in this class!" He told me that the course had been sold out for months, but someone had canceled and opened up a spot for me just minutes before I called.

I arrived on the first morning of ATP class both excited and nervous. Doreen came out before the event started and moved through the rows of chairs to personally greet everyone. When she made it to me, she took my hand and said, "Hi! I'm Doreen . . ." and suddenly stopped midsentence and just stared at me, still holding my hand and smiling. Then she repeated, "Hi, I'm Doreen. Who are *you*?"

Have you ever had an experience where you meet someone for the first time but feel as though you've known them *before*? That's exactly what I was experiencing with Doreen. It was a past-life moment, for sure.

The ATP course was five and a half days of sheer, absolute bliss. I went on to have one of the most life-changing experiences of my life at ATP. My skills as a reader were taken to the next level! ATP opened my eyes to aspects of spirituality that I had been blind to before taking the course. My interactions with Joshua and especially the archangels increased dramatically afterward.

I followed up the course with many more classes with Doreen, then began working with her as a staff member at her events. She quickly became my mentor, my sister, and my friend. I know in my heart that our relationship is so close and easy because she has been my mentor in many lifetimes.

Nearly everything I know about angels, I learned from the "angel lady," Doreen. Her path as a teacher and mentor has continued to grow to reach many other students. She became a born-again Christian in early 2017 after having a deeply moving Jesus experience, and her work with angels also began to shift at that point.

Your earthly mentors aren't the only ones who will be assisting you in reaching your magical life. Heaven will also send you magical helpers: *angels*.

Angel Public Relations

There are several kinds of angels, and the two you'll want to interact with the most are *guardian angels* and *archangels*. If you want to learn all about the angels, there's an endless amount of information out there, filling many volumes. In this book, however, I'll be focusing on the aspects of angels that I've found to be most useful for living a magical life.

All angels require that you first ask for their assistance, except in certain life-threatening circumstances. Although your guardian angels never leave your side, if you want their help with a particular situation, life goal, or challenge, you need to request it.

I suggest that everyone start their day with prayer and ask their angels for assistance that day. (As Doreen is always quick to point out, we pray to God, but we *talk* to our angels. I talk to my angels in a very meditative way, but it's not the same as prayer.) I always ask my guardian angels for help each day, and I also ask archangels for help based on their particular specialties as they relate to whatever I have going on.

Archangels tend to get all the best press, but guardian angels are very special. So it's surprising to me the number of people who sort of skip over their guardian angels when asking for help and go straight to the archangel realm. It's partially because information about archangels is more popular. They have specific names and assignments that have been extensively written about. Some are even listed as saints in the Catholic tradition.

Even I quickly got dazzled by the amazing and oh-so-magical archangels when I began on my spiritual path. I was particularly charmed by Archangel Uriel, with his glittery, sparkling, golden light. I wrote books and created angel cards with the help of coppery Archangel Gabriel, danced in the joyful fuchsia light of Archangel Jophiel, and felt the royal blue protection of Archangel Michael.

However, over the last few years, my focus has returned to guardian angels. You could even say I've become a sort of public relations guy for the guardian angels!

I love guardian angels. I mean, they *know* me. They really, really *know* me. Heck, I'm sure they know me far better than I even know myself.

They see every last kooky thing you do and are there with an angelic high five for every brilliant or loving act. When you're in a time of challenge, they know you need them before you ever utter the first prayerful word. Archangels are fantastic and I totally adore them, but it's your guardian angels who are on the front lines of your life.

GETTING TO KNOW YOUR GUARDIAN ANGELS

Everyone comes into this world with at least two guardian angels who are with you from birth until death. The information I've received says that they're then with you life after life (through each reincarnation). They know you better than you know yourself, and their love is infinite and unconditional.

Your guardian angels are among the most precious friends you can possibly have. They're there for you day and night . . . never, ever leaving your side. You're their sole focus, and they love you beyond what any words could ever express.

It's rare to experience the voice of an angel in the same way you would that of a friend. It's more of an inner hearing. If you *see* angels, it's likely you're actually "seeing" them through your mind's eye.

Each person usually has one primary guardian angel, who is the easiest to hear. In my experience working with both my own and other people's guardian angels, the primary one tends to focus on comforting you and making you feel safe and loved. The other guardian angels around most often have specific tasks or areas of expertise in your life. Those areas will change as, for example, you turn your focus from romance to career and life purpose.

Those who seek out their guardian angels have varying experiences. Some make the effort and figure out who all of their guardian angels are at once. Others, like me, may discover new angels around them as time goes by. For decades, I only knew about my primary guardian angel, Joshua. But in the last 10 years or so, I've become acquainted with two more.

I think of Joshua as my overall "no job too small, no task too big," "never fear, he's always here" total dear of an angel! The other two focus their work on particular areas of my life. The third angel I had no idea about until my coteacher discovered him for me while we were filming new material for the *Certified Angel Card Reader* course that we teach together. But once I knew he was there, I quickly knew why. My career was really starting to soar, and my newly discovered guardian angel quickly took over as my angelic agent, opening doors for me and giving me great advice on what to do next!

It's important to note here that our passed-over loved ones are *not* guardian angels. People often say that the dearly departed are watching over them, which is a beautiful and wonderful thing and very real. My mother passed away in 2013, and I've no doubt that she watches over me very closely and provides a helping hand in my life from time to time. She, along with other departed loved ones, is considered a spiritual guide. Guardian angels are with you from birth until you pass back into the Light. They may work closely with beloved family members or guides in Heaven, but they're not the same kind of soul.

Archangels are also not guardian angels. But just like spirit guides or beloved passed-over family members, they can hang out with you regularly. In fact, I feel the loving presence of Archangels Uriel and Gabriel constantly, but I'm not their sole focus. Guardian angels are focused solely on you, while archangels help billions of people at once every day.

What's in a Name?

People are always asking me what the names of their guardian angels are. For years and years, I refrained from presenting those names to them. In my mind, meeting Joshua was such a magical experience that I was afraid to deny anyone that experience on their own. However, that changed in the fall of 2015, during an episode of my radio show, *Magical Things with Radleigh Valentine.*

When a woman called my show and asked for the names of her guardian angels, I opened my mouth to say, "No, but let me tell you how to do it on your own." But the words didn't come out. Instead, I heard Joshua say, *Do it.*

In my mind, I answered back with, *What?*
Josh replied, *I said, just do it!*
So I did.

Immediately following that show, my Facebook page was so full of requests for guardian-angel names that I took it as a sign that it was time to start saying yes to that particular request. Joshua explains that it's a way to help people jump-start their relationship with their angels (and he is never wrong).

Your angels' names may be regular ones, like Joshua. Or they might be very strange-sounding names that you don't come across in daily life. They might sound biblical. It's also not uncommon for guardian angels to have the same names as archangels. When that happens, you'll need to get clarity by asking your angels whether they're the very famous archangels just wanting you to know that they're there for you, or if they're your guardian angels who just happen to also have those names.

My experience is that if your guardian angel has the same name as an archangel, it's because he or she has a purpose in your life similar to the archangel's specialty. It may also be a message from your guardian angel that you should be working with that archangel on a more regular basis.

The first and easiest way to find out your guardian angels' names is to just *ask*. Set the intention to meet your angels through meditation, lighting a candle, playing soft music . . . whatever matches your personal definition of being at peace for a few minutes. Your angels' names are usually the first ones that come into your mind. Don't let your ego tell you you're making it up.

You can also ask your angels for validation that you got the name right. That "proof" usually takes the form of coming across that name over and over in the following days. This may also lead to clearing up any misunderstanding about your angel's name. For example, if you received the name Ava for your angel, but all week long the name Eva crops up, then you might want to check in with your angel again to see if Eva is actually the right name.

Another thing you can do is ask your angels for a sign. This often results in the same experience I just mentioned; you'll just keep bumping into a name as the days pass. Or perhaps you repeatedly see roses, indicating that your guardian angel's name is Rose.

Another great way to get an angel's name is through Doreen's *Messages from Your Angels Oracle Cards*. Each of the 44 cards in the deck has an angel's name written on it. Focus on your request to know your guardian angel's name while shuffling the cards. When you pull a card—*voilà!*—you have one of your guardian angels' names.

HEARING THE NAME OF JOSHUA

I first learned the name of my primary guardian angel back in the late '90s. I had recently moved into a new home and noticed that there was something a little different about the energy. Sometimes I would "bump into" something that wasn't there in the house. I specifically remember walking down a hallway one day with a basket of freshly folded laundry and feeling as though I had bumped into *someone*. I immediately threw the laundry—basket and all—into the air!

Oh great, I thought. *I've moved into a haunted house. Isn't that just swell?*

I recounted this story shortly thereafter to a very wise, insightful friend. Her response was, "Well, you're the angel boy. What makes you think it's something bad? Did it ever occur to you that it's one of your feathered friends?"

At the time, I was very much into my spirituality and trying to learn about angels and other aspects of the Divine. As it turns out, there really wasn't anything different about the energy in the house. There was something different about the energy in *me*. My personal spiritual work was starting to bear fruit! I was so ready to have a more up-close-and-personal relationship with my angels that I was bumping into their energy in my home.

One day, I walked into my bedroom, sat down on the edge of my bed, and looked at the painting of a guardian angel on the wall. (Called *Watchers in the Night*, by Thomas Blackshear, it's still precious to me.) I didn't do anything fancy. I just looked at the picture and said, "You seem to know me, and I would really like to get to know you. So let's just start with: What's your name?"

Now, I know I told you that it is highly unusual to literally hear an angel's voice. It's typically something you sort of hear in your head. But in this case, loud and clear—as if a human were speaking to me—I heard "Joshua."

I was so stunned that I just looked at the painting and said, "You know, I think that that'll do it for today." Then I left the room!

That night, I had a vivid "dream" about Joshua. I put the word *dream* in quotation marks because at first I thought I *was* dreaming, but it became something so much more. In the dream, I encountered Joshua, and it felt like having accidentally run into your closest, most beloved friend after not having seen him for years and years. We were both laughing and crying and hugging each other. It was in that moment that I became "awake" within the dream and thought, *Wait a minute! This isn't a dream—this is really happening!*

Even 20 years later, recounting this poignant story puts tears in my eyes. This was the beginning of a long and treasured relationship and conversation with Joshua, my other guardian angels, and eventually the archangels.

WHO YA GONNA CALL?
ARCHANGELS!

There are countless archangels protecting this world as well as other worlds. However, there are 15 well-known archangels, and among them, the most commonly known are the "big four": *Gabriel, Michael, Raphael,* and *Uriel.*

As I mentioned before, the archangels are very popular. And why not? They're sort of like the superstars of the angelic realm. They have very specific roles that are simple to understand, so it's easy to see why people gravitate toward them. It's straightforward enough to say to yourself, "I have a health problem. Time to call Archangel Raphael," or, "I don't feel safe; better call Archangel Michael."

Each archangel has a specialty. That's not to say that any of them wouldn't happily help you in any way they could on *any* issue, but they still have their primary focuses. For example, you can call Archangel Michael for health issues, and he'd do his best to support you. However, given that his specialty is cutting your connections to the past and keeping you safe, he'd probably try to help you in that way. So, it's a bit like calling a carpenter to address your plumbing problem.

Before I briefly introduce you to each of the 15 most prominent archangels and their specialties, it's important to understand that angels don't really have genders. However, their specialties— along with the energy they give out—tend to feel male or female to most people. The gender that I use for each of the archangels is the one most commonly associated with that angel. However, if you see them differently, then that's what's perfect for you and you should allow that to be.

- *Archangel Ariel:* If you're concerned with manifesting what you need in this world from the standpoint of abundance, prosperity, or your material needs, Ariel is your gal. She's also the protector of nature, including animals and the environment. Her name translates as "the lioness of God," and she is associated with the color pale pink.

- *Archangel Azrael:* If you're burdened with sorrow, have suffered a loss, or are in need of comfort and a way to get past what you've experienced, call upon Azrael. He is the most graceful and the most elegant of all the archangels. His name means "the mercy of God," and he can help you or those you know in need find comfort. He is known for appearing in a creamy-white color.

- *Archangel Chamuel:* If you've lost something or are searching for something (the perfect job, the perfect mate, your car keys), Archangel Chamuel can come to your aid. His name means "the eyes of God," and he can help you find anything you're looking for. Resonating in a pale green color, he's also the archangel to call if you're trying to come to peace about something in your life.

- *Archangel Gabriel:* Archangel Gabriel is much like the patron archangel of creative people. If you are working on something artistic; are a creative type like an actor, a speaker, or a writer; or need to find the right words for a conversation, then Archangel Gabriel is perfect for you. She is also great if you need someone to help push you past procrastination and get stuff done. As she is the angel of the Annunciation, she is also known to work with people regarding pregnancy, birth, or adoption. Her associated color is copper, and her name means "the strength of God."

- *Archangel Haniel:* Archangel Haniel's name means the "grace of God." If your concern is about growing your spiritual gifts and becoming more intuitive, then ask for her assistance. She can help with giving readings or doing them for yourself. She also specializes in women's issues. She is known to appear in a silvery blue color.

- *Archangel Jeremiel:* Jeremiel is another archangel who's awesome for developing your spiritual gifts, but who is also great at helping you review your life to date so that you can understand what changes you need to make. His name means "the mercy of God," and his color is deep purple.

- *Archangel Jophiel:* Archangel Jophiel is the archangel of beauty. She can help you clean up your space and beautify any part of your life. Some call her the feng shui angel. I prefer to think of her as the archangel of positive thinking, because you can also call on her if your thoughts need cleaning up. As you might suspect, her name means "the beauty of God," and she resonates to a fuchsia pink.

- *Archangel Metatron:* If you need help with time management, then Archangel Metatron will be of assistance. He can bend time for you so that you have more time to get a project done or arrive somewhere on time even if you left later than you meant to. He's also known as the protector of children and very sensitive people. The meaning of his name is unclear. His color is a blend of violet and green.

- *Archangel Michael:* For those who are feeling unsafe, I recommend asking for the help of Archangel Michael, "he who is like God." Known for helping protect us and also soothing our fears, Michael can sever unwanted connections to the past or to people you feel need to be safely and lovingly removed from your life. If you need self-confidence or clarity on your life purpose, call upon Michael. His color is a deep royal blue, sometimes seen with a hint of gold.

- *Archangel Raguel:* If your concern is clearing up an argument, resolving a misunderstanding, or just making sure that things go well among individuals or groups, Raguel is the right one to call. His name means "the friend of God," and he can smooth over difficult interpersonal situations or even help you make new friends. His color is a pale, robin's-egg blue.

- *Archangel Raphael:* Raphael, whose name means "God heals," is the archangel for physical healing. So if you're sick, in physical pain, or have other bodily ailments, he's your guy. Raphael is also the archangel of safe travels, so you can call upon him while flying or driving long distances. He is also known as a bit of a matchmaker. I often suggest that people work with Raphael and Chamuel in partnership for issues of finding the right romantic partner. Raphael's healing light is emerald green.

- *Archangel Raziel:* I always think of Raziel as a kind of wizard of the archangel realm. He's very magical and can help you understand esoteric information, heal from past-life issues, or interpret your nighttime dreams. His name means "the secrets of God," as he is said to sit at the throne of God, writing down all he hears. He radiates rainbow colors.

- *Archangel Sandalphon:* When you feel as though your prayers aren't being heard or are being left unanswered, you can call upon Sandalphon, the archangel known to personally carry prayers to God. Ask him for help seeing, hearing, or knowing what the answers to your prayers are. He's also the archangel associated with music, so musicians should take heed! Sandalphon means "brother together," and he appears turquoise in color.

- *Archangel Uriel:* Do you need a brilliant idea? Are you seeking a true epiphany about what to do next or any aspect of your life? Then Archangel Uriel is there for you. Uriel is also known for emotional healing, so if you carry pain from the past you need to reconcile and work through, he can help. Along with Gabriel, he's a great archangel to work with if you see yourself as a spiritual teacher. His name means "the light of God." I see him as being a glittery golden color, though others perceive him as solid yellow.

- *Archangel Zadkiel:* Zadkiel, "the righteousness of God," is the tutor of the archangel realm. Think of him as a kind of angelic ginkgo biloba! If your concern is taking tests, passing your exams in school, learning something new, or just remembering things, call upon Zadkiel, who is associated with deep indigo blue. He can also help you with forgiveness of yourself and others.

If this type of information fascinates you as much as it does me, I would highly recommend you read Doreen's book *Archangels 101.*

ANGELIC APPEARANCES

Many years ago, I attended a particularly memorable angel conference. The speaker had prepared a meditation to introduce us to the 15 most well-known archangels. I was very much looking forward to this, as my intuitive gifts were really ramping up, so I anticipated a vivid experience.

The speaker began inviting the archangels into the room in alphabetical order, starting with Ariel. To my surprise, the experience was completely flat to me. I shuffled in my seat to get more comfortable and tried to really focus on the meditation. Next came Azrael and then Chamuel. Still, I felt like I was in the auditorium by myself. I wasn't feeling anything and wondered what was wrong.

The speaker went through all the archangels, and I continued to feel nothing until she got to the 14th, Uriel. Suddenly the room exploded into glitters of golden light! I could hear angels singing! The sparkling light was almost blinding to me, and I felt euphoric. I was amazed by what I was experiencing.

When the speaker brought up the final archangel, Zadkiel, the entire meditation went completely black again.

Later that same day, I pulled a card from an angel deck: "Archangel Uriel." Immediately afterward, another participant at the event pulled a card for me from a different deck; again, it featured Archangel Uriel. At the end of the day, one of the very gifted readers at the event came up to me to tell me that she saw Uriel with me.

Okay, okay! I get it! I thought.

Not all angel experiences are that powerful. (Frankly, I wish they were!) But if an angel really wants your attention, believe me—they will find a way to get it. I like to believe that Archangel Uriel put his golden glitter stamp on me so that I could teach the world bright, shiny new ideas.

Sometimes specific archangels tend to stay with you all the time, like Uriel does with me. Others may come to be with you just for a certain period of time to help you with something specific or because they have something that they want you to know.

It's important to note that the archangels are what we call "omnipresent." What that means is that they can be everywhere and anywhere at once. This is because archangels work on the same plane as God. (Most of the archangels' names end in *-el*, a suffix that means "of God.") They're not bound by the laws of humankind that restrict time and space. They're above that. Saying that an archangel is too busy to help you is like saying *God* is too busy to help you. So there's no need for you to worry that asking something of Archangel Michael, for example, would take him away from someone with a "greater" need, because he can simultaneously be with as many people as need his help.

MESSAGES FROM THE DIVINE

You don't need anyone's help to get messages from your angels. You can do it all by yourself. Similar to the process of getting the names of your guardian angels, you can set the intention to receive angelic communication through meditation, lighting a candle, playing soft music, and so forth. The messages will gently drift into your awareness. Your ego may try to convince you that it's all in your imagination, but that's not true.

If you believe you're getting unkind or judging messages, that's your ego talking, *not* your angels. Angels don't have egos of any kind. They'll never judge you. They'll never speak unkindly to you. Their messages will always be loving.

If meditation isn't your thing, a really great way to get messages from your angels is through automatic writing. This is how I first started getting them, and it's really easy. (I explain how to do that in the Genie Academy lesson at the end of this chapter.)

If you're having trouble believing the message, you can also ask your angels for evidence that you got it right and then watch for signs or synchronicities that validate what you received. Guardian angels often talk through signs. They might send you feathers or pennies or butterflies. A day might pass where you just keep seeing images of angels on billboards or television. You might see the number 4 all day long, which is a special number that means "angels are with you." If your angels are sending you signs, it's often because they want to get your attention so that they can have a much stronger relationship with you.

Angels will also present themselves to you in the way that you can most relate to. For example, you may perceive your angels as wearing white robes and having big white wings and golden halos. That's not at all uncommon, and that's how they'll show up if that's the way you need them to appear. My guardian angel Joshua, however, looks to me like an older brother who loves to tease me and laugh with me. Growing up the way I did, that's what I needed—someone to protect me and love me as an older brother would. I'm sure his appearance would change if I needed it to, but I don't need it to. I like him just the way he is.

Everyone is unique, so there are as many ways of talking to Heaven as there are people on Earth. No matter how closely you might follow a particular faith or spiritual practice, there's still going to be a little (or a lot!) of your own personal uniqueness that gets thrown in. The thing is, Heaven really doesn't care *how* you communicate, only that you *do*. You can tell the Divine your preference, and it will happily follow your lead!

Imagine for a moment that you're at a large international convention. The only language you speak is English. All around you people are conversing in French, German, Spanish, Japanese, Portuguese . . . you name it! It's a total fruit salad of messages coming at you, but you really can't understand a word being said. Of course, you could certainly learn French or Spanish or another language. But that would take quite a while.

Or you could just stop and say, "Could someone *please* speak English to me?!"

Well, Heaven is just like that! You can ask to be spoken to in signs; through meditation, angel cards, or automatic writing; or in whatever way you feel the most comfortable and confident getting the information.

SIGNS OF THE TIMES

Signs are a very powerful way to get messages from Heaven. But you have to really pay attention. Like I said, some of the most frequent signs from angels are white feathers, pennies, butterflies, and angel numbers. (I suggest reading *Angel Numbers 101*, another book by Doreen, for more information about all the specific meanings of numbers.)

The most common scenario I hear from people who want signs from their angels but who say they don't get anything goes like this . . .

> I get up in the morning. I take five seconds to meditate or just say a little something to my angels. *Just need a message today, please*, I ask. Then I hop into the shower and start running through 18 alternatives in my mind for how my workday will go, and what I need to do for the kids, and what's for dinner. I get in the car, drive like crazy to work, and try to accomplish as much as I can. I then pick up the kids, stop at the grocery store, make dinner, get the kids to bed, and finally collapse on the couch.

At the end of the day, these people are often wondering why their angels have let them down again. Then they call in to my radio show to ask me if they even *have* guardian angels. But where—I seriously ask you—in that scenario was there a moment when that poor person paused to notice any signs their angels may have been throwing them?

Because, in truth, the car in front of them had a license plate with the numbers 444 on it. (Recall that the number 4 means that your angels are with you.) They passed a billboard featuring an angel with open arms. The song "Calling All Angels" was playing softly on the radio on their way to pick up the kids, and they stepped over a white feather as they got out of their car when they got home.

But nope. No messages from their angels today.

I want to assure you that blessings from Heaven fall upon you every day, like raindrops in Seattle. The question is: Are you noticing? Or are you just grumbling about the rain?

I jokingly call myself a "symbolism nerd" because I find it all so fascinating. There are many volumes of books that talk about the symbolism of this or that. Some people who are very aware and notice a particular image or thing recurring in their life will use a search engine to get the meaning. For example, if you were to continually see images of giraffes over several days, you might go on the Internet and type in "symbolism giraffe" and receive your message that way.

However, it isn't necessary to learn all about symbolism to receive signs from the angels. To get messages from Heaven through signs, you just have to notice *everything*. I find meaning in the simplest of gestures. Do I always understand the meaning? No, of course not. But I'm always trying, and after years of paying attention, I do get the meaning in most things.

Very recently, I found a piece of clothing that I hadn't seen in probably 10 years. I noticed that there was something in one of the pockets, so I pulled it out. It was a pack of spearmint gum. Now, I really dislike spearmint gum—spearmint *anything*, really. And yet, I knew immediately how it must have gotten there. And in that moment, it was a very powerful message to me. Poignant, sweet, and extremely meaningful. Suddenly I found myself in the highly unlikely scenario of holding a decade-old pack of spearmint gum to my heart.

On occasion, the angels will send you a whole series of signs that you simply can't ignore. It's sort of like a gentle angel whomp on the head! For example, a few years ago, Lee and I were driving around town doing errands when he suddenly shouted, "Oh my God! Look at that car!"

The car in question was stunning. It was a fiery red and orange color I had never seen before, and it blazed in the sun. I'm really into cars and especially fascinated by their colors. I've saved stacks of car "color chips" all the way back to 1957. So once we were home, I went on the Internet to search for that color because my car "color curiosity" had gotten the best of me.

It was surprisingly hard to track down the color, as it was brand-new to the model. I found the car and discovered that there were only 4 (an angel number!) in that color in the country. One of the cars I found online had just been traded in after having been driven for only 777 miles. (In angel numbers, 777 means: "You're on the right path. Keep going.")

Interesting, I thought.

Out of curiosity, I added up the vehicle identification number (VIN), which I always do for cars that I'm thinking about purchasing. Now, mind you, I wasn't really thinking of buying this car. I wasn't in the market for a new one, and this car was crazy expensive. I also liked my current car. It was only four years old, with 14,000 miles on it, and I planned on keeping it for years and years. Still, just for fun, I went ahead and did the math and got 8—the number of abundance. Basically, I just took each digit of the VIN and added them together. In this case, the number added up to 35, the two digits of which I then added together to get 8! This is the number I always like the VIN of the cars I buy to add up to.

Right about then, I looked down at my feet and there was a white feather. Now, please keep in mind I was sitting in my living room. Not outside. Not at a café. In my living room. How does a white feather just mysteriously show up in your living room?

So now, even I (Mr. Magic) was starting to be a little freaked out. I thought about turning off my computer and forgetting the whole thing, but my guardian angel Josh kept saying, "Keep looking!"

I sighed deeply and said to my angels, "Okay. Fine. You better know what you're doing here."

I e-mailed the dealership, which was in another state. It was Easter Sunday, so I was sure I wouldn't hear anything until at least Monday. But no. Right away I got an e-mail back from a guy named Michael. (You know. *Like the archangel?*)

Okay. Feather at my feet. E-mail from Michael. My little freakarama continued to grow.

Michael told me that the car had been purchased by a man for his wife, but she found the car not to her liking, so they traded it back in after just three months.

There were too many signs to ignore. Reluctantly, I headed out the next day to a dealership in my own city to drive a car that was just like it, although in a different color. When I sat down in the car to test-drive it, I saw that the odometer read: 1,444. The number of angels. They're with me. (This angel number is a message about staying optimistic and to let the angels help you with your fears.)

I asked the salesperson, "Why does this car have so few miles on it?"

He said, "Oh, we sold this car to a guy, and he traded it back to us after just three months because something he wanted more showed up on our lot." Same story as the car with the 777 miles on it in another state! *Seriously?*

As you might suspect, by this time I was just laughing. Then, while leaving the lot, I got a call on my cell phone telling me that Hay House had just approved my fifth project with them. As I was getting the information about my new contract, a car in that fiery color drove past me. Then, when I got home, I found an unexpected check in the mail.

I didn't need a new car. I wasn't inclined to buy a new car. Although none of this made the slightest sense to me, by my count that was 10 signs from my angels within a 24-hour period telling me to buy this car. That's just not something you can ignore, so I bought the car, and I love it!

I still don't know exactly why I needed it, but I got a hint when a friend of mine told me she felt the fiery color was more visible and safer than the beige car I had. If that's the case, then perhaps I averted an accident that I will never know about by listening to my angels.

Of course, the way I explain this story, it sounds like a total "Well, duh, Rad! I wish all signs were that easy." The truth is, most of them *are*. If I had just blown off the first one or two synchronicities, I would never have had so many pile up like a metaphorical trail of bread crumbs. The overwhelming message to buy the car would have been lost. That's why it's so important to stay awake to the messages of signs and to give each one special attention.

Another thing you need to know is that the angels and Heaven are very efficient. I mean, like, *very efficient!* Not too long ago a friend of mine sent me a picture of an image that to her looked like Archangel Jophiel. To me, it appeared to be Archangel Gabriel. Indeed, *both* archangels made sense for her particular situation. By showing it to me, she allowed Heaven to make the one image have multiple correct meanings. On top of that, by showing it to me, *I* got a message that I needed from Archangel Gabriel. So don't allow human perception to let you think a message must only mean one thing, and only be for one person. Don't underestimate Heaven's magical ability to help many people at once.

The way in which you ask an angel for a sign also matters, especially if you're just getting the knack of this. Make things easy on your angels. Don't make your queries too complicated, such as, "Angels, I need to know whether I should move to either Detroit, Chicago, or some other city." While the angels could send you an answer, you might not see the message if you're a newbie.

For your *own* sake, set up your requests in either-or and if-then statements. For example, you might say: "Angels, if I'm supposed to move to Chicago, then send me simple and easy-to-notice signs that you're with me on this." Over the course of the day, look for feathers, pennies, doves, and the like. If you see none, then tomorrow ask the angels the same question about Detroit. If you see feathers galore, start packing! If you see nothing, then ask your angels on the third day if there's somewhere else you should move to.

Later, as you get better at noticing signs, you can ask more open-ended questions, and somehow images of Chicago or people who are from Chicago or subtle references to Chicago will be easy for you to see. And then you'll know!

As time goes by, you'll also discover special signs that angels use just for you. Maybe you'll smell roses where none appear to be present. Or, just finding yourself near roses when it's an oddity for you to be in their vicinity could be a message!

Open your heart to the possibilities. Open your mind to the idea that big messages can be found in little things (like a pack of spearmint gum).

Open your eyes to the magic. Because it's beautiful. And it's waiting for you.

It's in the Cards

Without question, the biggest impediment to recognizing messages from angels, signs from Heaven, or even answers to prayers is the ego. The ego wants you to believe that God is big and judgmental and mad as can be at you—and you're small, flawed, insignificant, and nothing special. The ego says, "Oh puh-lease! Why would God bother with you? Of course you can't hear your angels; you have no gifts. Oh, and by the way, there *are* no angels."

My response to your ego is: "Liar, liar, pants on fire!"

God is big. That's about the only part of that narrative that's true. God is grand and loving and expansive and so proud of you that there are simply no words to express it. You, on the other hand, are also grand and loving and incredibly magical and deserving. Unless you've been studying your entire life, you undoubtedly have spiritual gifts you can't begin to comprehend—and *yes*, you have angels. Both God and those loving, devoted, always-at-your-side, adoring angels can't wait to talk to you! As I've already explained, Heaven is very chatty. It's always talking to you.

Still, wrestling the ego to the ground can be quite challenging, for some more than others. That's why over time highly spiritual people have developed specialized ways to communicate with the Divine that can get around the ego. One of those ways is angel oracle cards and tarot cards. (At the time of this writing, I've written five tarot decks and one oracle card deck, so I know a lot about this topic.) You can think of these cards as being like a "telephone to Heaven" or "God's hotline."

There are a couple of reasons why cards and other divinatory tools work:

1. First of all, the ego is constantly beating you up, but when you use cards, you're putting your faith in them and their connection to Heaven. Either consciously or unconsciously, you see

them as magical, and the pressure is off you to be the source of the Divine messages that come through.

While cards *are* magical, they aren't the source of the message. *God* is. These cards just help you get your ego out of the way enough for you to allow the Divine messages to be delivered. They're fun to work with, but in the end, you don't *need* them to get messages from Heaven. Remember that *you*—not the pictures in front of you—are the one connected to the Divine, receiving messages.

2. Another reason why divinatory tools work is best explained by analogy. Imagine a beautiful forest that people have walked through for hundreds, even thousands, of years. Naturally, people would choose the most efficient (and maybe most scenic) route through the forest. What develops is a well-worn path that has been tread by millions and millions of people. People have faith in that path and trust that it's the perfect way through the forest. In a similar way, millions and millions of people have put their faith in those cards or divinatory tools for hundreds, even thousands, of years. Imagine the combined Genie magic that has been invested in that way of speaking to the Divine! Can you comprehend how powerful that is? You can trust the cards to be a magical path leading you through the forest of spirituality right to Heaven.

A lot of people have been frightened by tarot cards in the past. I get that. I was none too pleased, either, by much of the imagery and words on the cards. There's a card in tarot that traditionally shows a poor guy lying facedown in a pool of blood with 10 swords in his back. Well, *ew*. We don't need that kind of gore just to get the message, "Hey. This situation has come to an end."

I see it as part of my life purpose to remove the "tarot-fying" parts of tarot by bringing the cards up to date to match the sensitive nature of people on Earth today. We can get that same message with imagery that's more poignant and meaningful.

Frankly, I consider it part of my life purpose to take the fear out of spirituality in general, not just tarot. It helps to remember that the imagery and words on ancient tarot cards harken back to a time when life itself was pretty frightening. People were more accustomed to the frightening imagery on tarot cards because it was pretty close to what life was like. While life on Earth right now is nowhere near perfect, it's still a lot better than it used to be. We have evolved. Our souls have grown to be more sensitive and more spiritual.

Tarot mirrors life, and there are sad times that come in life. I didn't remove those experiences from tarot. But I did make the imagery and words more accessible to people so as not to scare them to death. I tweaked tarot to match the sensitive natures of the people currently living on Earth.

With nothing left to scare us, what remains is a beautiful, insightful, and magical way to shove the ego aside and talk to God.

* *

GENIE ACADEMY

Lesson #7: Talking to Your Guardian Angels

A great method to start getting messages or the names of your angels is *automatic writing*. I suggest that you dedicate a journal or notebook solely to your angel messages. As in meditation, find a peaceful space and time for your writing where you won't be interrupted. I like to start with a little prayer. I'm using the word *God*, but as always, use whatever term fits your faith.

Dear God,

I am very excited to begin a deeper relationship with You through communicating with the angels. Please send the perfect guardian angels or archangels to speak with me. Allow the messages to come through clearly and easily. Please help push my ego aside so that I can receive the information with full faith that it's Divine in nature and perfect for helping me at this time. I ask that You send Archangel Michael to surround and protect me and this space during this time of angelic communication. And so it is . . .

I like to go about automatic writing like a conversation. If you don't know the names of your guardian angels, then you might want to begin by introducing yourself and asking them to do the same, just as I did when I first met Joshua. If you do know the names of your angels, then you can either start by writing a hello to one of them, or something along the lines of: "Hi, this is Kathy. Who wants to talk today?" This allows your guardian angels (or perhaps even an archangel) to decide who has the most pertinent message for you in that moment.

Ask your question, then write down the answer as it comes to you. Don't edit, and don't rethink it. Just write freely, letting your hand move across the page without trying to direct it. The answers probably won't sound like your voice and won't use words you tend to use. Over time, you'll also start to recognize the differences between the ways each of your guardian angels speak, and you'll know immediately without asking who's communicating with you.

Remember, if the answers are harsh, judgmental, or unkind, you're in your ego. When this happens, ask Archangel Michael to clear that energy from your conversation, tear out the page to remove the ego-based conversation from your journal, and throw it away so that you can begin fresh.

In time, you won't need the journal. You'll just be able to start up a conversation with your angels in your private space, in the car, while going for a walk, or just about anywhere!

✦ ✦ ✦

Lesson #8: Archangel Prescriptions

Many years ago, I discovered a way of working with the angels when I needed their help that I've found to be amazingly simple, effective, and supportive. I call this method "Archangel Prescriptions."

Imagine yourself standing in a room or out in nature. Envision four angels surrounding you, forming a square, with you being the magical person in the middle. (Remember that 4 is the number that represents angels.)

Now choose the angels for whatever situation you want help with. If you're just looking to have your angels' general protection and companionship for the day, you might select two archangels to stand before you and two of your guardian angels behind you. For topics you consider to be very important to you, opt for four archangels.

The key is to let your intuition guide you as to which archangels you ask to walk with you and which of the four positions to place them in. I initiate every walk with my angels by asking for Archangel Uriel's help. Many people simply wouldn't go anywhere without Archangel Michael.

Since Archangel Michael is known for safety and protection, you might choose him as one of the archangels blazing a trail in front of you. If you're feeling as though other people might not be being as honest or kind as you deserve, you might choose to put your guardian angels in front of you so that you know that Archangel Michael has "got your back." Then, if you're having trouble staying optimistic, you might want your fourth angel to be Archangel Jophiel. She can help you to see the positive in every situation by beautifying your thoughts. Think of her as angelic rose-colored glasses (but only in the most supportive of ways) for more serious situations.

Let's look at some other examples of groupings of archangels for specific topics. Say that you're looking to find a romantic partner. One possible group of archangels you might ask to walk with you would be Raphael, Chamuel, Jophiel, and Raguel. Archangel Raphael is known to have done some matchmaking in ancient texts. Chamuel can see anything and everything, so he knows exactly where the perfect match for you is and how to make your paths cross. Archangel Jophiel can help you to remain positive and create a beautiful experience for everyone. Archangel Raguel can make things go smoothly and assure that everyone is being open and honest about their feelings.

If your concern is career or life purpose, you might start with Ariel, the archangel of abundance and prosperity. Add in Archangel Jeremiel, who specializes in life reviews, to help you understand where you've been and where you are now in order to get a grasp on where you want to go. Then consider including Archangel Michael, known for helping people understand their life purpose, and Uriel, the archangel of great ideas and epiphanies who also helps make you stand out in a crowd.

Of course, these aren't the only groupings of archangels that can be created. Take a moment now to come up with lists of whom you might call upon for each situation in your life.

✦ ✦ ✦

Lesson #9: Your Angelic Alphabet

One of the most powerful ways in which angels will speak to you is through signs. Remember, however, that there's no need to learn all about the meaning of specific symbols to receive signs from the angels. Think of signs as a language of their own, with each symbol representing a letter of your angelic alphabet. The Universe is very happy to talk to you in any way you want it to, so you can also create your own symbolism. For example, my mom loved pink roses and owls, so my sister and I have come to see pink roses or owls that pop up unexpectedly as signs that our mother is sending her love.

In this lesson, you're going to make a list of signs that you would like the Universe to use when communicating with you. It's best if the symbols you choose aren't things that you see every day. If you are a lover of orchids and your home is full of them, then it might not be a very effective symbol for you to give to Heaven to use.

Also, don't make it extremely difficult for the angels to use your alphabet. If you live somewhere very warm where it never snows, a snowflake might not be such a great choice (though it's not impossible!). Conversely, you don't have to live in Africa to have an elephant as a sign. Your angels may just show you elephants painted on coffee cups or in magazine ads. You might also want to incorporate some traditional signs into your alphabet. I've already noted that feathers, coins, and butterflies are very common signs that your angels are with you and want you to know they love you and wish to communicate with you.

Take some time now to create your angelic alphabet of signs. Write down each sign you want the Universe to use and what it means to you. Then ask the Divine to use your alphabet to talk to you! Over time, the list will expand as you get better at paying attention to the messages you're getting.

CHAPTER 6

DAILY MAGIC

This chapter is about what I call "daily magic." This isn't magic with the aim of manifesting anything in particular or granting specific wishes—although practicing doing so will certainly help! Daily magic is more about keeping you in the energy of living a magical life all the time.

The following are things that I suggest you practice every day when possible. This has two benefits:

- **First**, it keeps you in a place of joy, hope, and faith.

- That in turn brings about the **second** benefit of keeping your wish-making skills primed and ready for use at any moment.

STAY AWAKE

We spoke a little bit in Chapter 1 about the concept of being awake. It's about being aware in the moment, which in my experience doesn't usually happen for most people while they're standing in line at the grocery store. The moment isn't something you're usually conscious of when doing the laundry, talking to a customer on the phone at work, or picking up the kids at school. Most of that's autopilot. It's akin to slumber.

Being awake is that moment when, for a split second, you know who you are. You remember how astonishingly beautiful you are. You see that life is a gift full of unending opportunities. Usually, epiphanies great and small pop into your mind.

In the movie *Joe Versus the Volcano*, the character Patricia tells Joe that almost the whole world is asleep. Only a few people are awake, she says, and these people live in a constant state of total amazement. Well, if that isn't a perfect, cosmic truth, I don't know what is! I love everything about that line. Think about being in constant, total amazement . . . that's the magic of life, right? Being awake and therefore able to see all the amazing beauty of every person and everything around you is what being your own Genie is all about.

When I want to make sure that I'm awake, what I do is focus on things that I believe are magic. I try to slow down time and just *be*. That may mean going outside and just standing in the yard or in a park. It can be meditating or having a chat with my angels. It might mean sitting with my pooch Jace and looking into his soulful brown eyes and asking him, "Whatcha wanna tell me today, fella?"

Just do anything to snap you out of the reverie of daily life. I think doing that at least once or twice a day can change your life. I'm serious. The insights you get can really keep you on track.

I'm not sure if it's possible to be awake *every single moment*. If it is, then I'll honestly tell you that it's not something I personally have mastered. There's just "stuff" that has to get done in this life on Earth, and some of it gets done via autopilot. But I do have a few helpful hints to make even mundane things more magical!

BIBBITY-BOBBITY-BOO

Daily magic means envisioning that there's magical energy in everything you do:

- Sweeping the floor? Imagine that as you sweep you're pushing all negative energy out of your house.

- Making a meal? With every ingredient you add, picture in your mind's eye that little magical sparkles of good health are being incorporated into the recipe.

- Getting dressed? Infuse magical elements into your clothing. Select colors that make you happy or wear sparkly jewelry or shoes. They don't have to be expensive, just a little magical!

I also recommend choosing a magical word for yourself—a word whose sole purpose is to help you to snap out of negative thinking or to wake you back up to the magic of life. When you feel like you're not having a very magical day, say the word and think of something happy. If you do this often enough, then the word itself will be all you need to get a magical boost to your day!

Speaking of magical words, don't forget those two I've already taught you: *yes* and *no*. I highly urge you to learn to use these two magical words very carefully.

Say yes to:

- Your dreams

- Things that give you joy

- Love

Say no to:

- Things that take you off course from your life purpose

- Things that make you unhappy

- Abuse, or people who take advantage of your kindness or giving nature

- Lovely and sincerely offered opportunities, if saying yes would simply be too much

A Prayer Is a Wish Your Heart Makes

Prayer is magical. If you've had a challenging time with religion in your past (like me), then don't even think of prayer as related to religion. Instead, think of it as your hotline to Heaven! This is you "texting" the Divine. This is posting a picture of your life on Instagram and tagging it with @God so your Creator sees it.

Personally, I've found music really clicks me into the magic of it all. I've been praying to the same meditation music for years now. However, if I don't happen to have that song with me, I still pray to something meditational or New Age.

Prayer is powerful for two reasons:

1. First of all, "If you don't ask, you don't get." That's a quote my grandmother often said, and she was absolutely right. Prayer is asking, and asking creates opportunities for Heaven to give you what you want. Your requests may come in bits and pieces, but they *do* come—or something better comes in their place.

2. When the good things show up, your confidence in yourself and your ability to create the world you want to manifest shoots right up!

I grew up in a church that excelled at guilt. Unfortunately, there was a lot of fear-based teaching and judging going on. As you might suspect, that didn't work so great for me. When I was old enough to control my own destiny, I walked out of organized religion in search of my own connection with the Divine. It didn't take me long to find it, either. It was just sort of there for me. It was as if a couple of angels were sitting on a park bench reading newspapers and I just walked up to hear one of them say, "Ah, good! There you are. We've been waiting."

It has taken me a long time to come to the place where I can say that I believe that organized religion is like anything else in this world: It can be a blessing, or it can be . . . *not* a blessing. And so when I walked away from something that was doing me true emotional harm, I suppose I may have thrown the baby out with the bathwater. That is to say, I was young, so I figured that if any part of something was bad, then it must *all* be bad.

One of those things I threw out with the bathwater was prayer. Curiously, it wasn't really the practice of prayer that I dispensed with, but the word itself. Since I was someone who would grow up to be an author and speaker, maybe it shouldn't be too surprising that I felt I needed a new vocabulary for my spirituality when I left organized religion.

God became the "Universe," the "Divine," or "Source." Prayer became my "daily meditations." Po-*tay*-to, po-*tah*-to. Right?

The healing of all that tiptoeing around theological vocabulary really started for me back in 1996 when I came across an amazing book, *Conversations with God*, by Neale Donald Walsch. It turned everything upside down for me. Well, actually, maybe I should say it turned everything upside *right* for me. Suddenly, God was out of the box. And that's when I got the word *God* back.

Getting the word *prayer* back is a more recent development for me. To be honest, it pretty much just amounted to me "getting over myself" as much as anything. The fact of the matter is, I never stopped praying. I just called it something else. To-*may*-to, to-*mah*-to.

Now please don't misunderstand me. As I've already said, I truly don't believe in my heart that there's one bit of difference between *God, Universe, Source,* and *Divine*—they're all synonyms for the same thing. Just as my "daily meditations" were just prayers.

But whether you know them as meditations or prayers, they're extremely important in our magical lives. They give us connection to the Divine. They allow us ways to express our hopes and our fears—our gratitude and our desires. They remind us that we, too, are of the Divine. We're magical children of God. And how cool is that?

So when it feels to us that our prayers aren't being heard . . . if we feel that our requests are unfulfilled . . . it can make us feel cut off from the magic. And that's not cool.

All our prayers are answered. The problem is that we may not recognize the answers, especially if they're different from the kind of answering we were envisioning. So here are my five easy steps to getting answers to your prayers—*and* noticing the response you get.

1. Know what you're praying for, but also be open to something better.

I think that people often get it in their minds that things have to be a certain way. And it's important to have what you're asking for crystal clear in your mind, but why wouldn't you want God to bring you something better if that's available? Whether it's a relationship, a career change, or the answer to a question, have it clearly articulated in your mind when you pray. Be in faith that the answer will come and that you'll know it when you see it. Then end your prayers by saying that you accept "this or something better," and *mean it.*

2. Be awake to answers that are different from what you're expecting or that come in a way that's different from what you anticipated.

Now I know this sounds a little like the last bit I just brought up, but there really is a difference. And the difference is in the noticing.

Let's say you prayed and asked God for a duck. (Hey, just work with me here, okay?) Maybe the duck is a sign to you; I don't know. But in any event, if you're so focused on asking for a duck that all you do is look and look and look for a duck, and nowhere can you see a duck, then you're going to be pretty sure that your prayers for a duck went unanswered—even as you trip over that swan standing right in front of you.

Most of the people who tell me that their prayers go unanswered simply don't have their eyes open to the crystal clear answer God just sent, even if it was better than what they were expecting.

3. Pray with gratitude, not with fear or begging.

Gratitude is a very important part of prayer. Praying with fear or in a begging sort of way is pretty much just convincing yourself that nothing is going to happen. You're closing your eyes to the answers Heaven is sending you. On the other hand, gratitude is a very open-eyed and expectant emotion. Pray with the faith and certainty that your answer will come in the perfect way and in the perfect time. When that happens, give thanks.

By the way, if patience isn't your strong suit, ask God to send you some intermediary signs or answers that the *big* answer to your prayers is coming. And then trust that!

4. Let Archangel Sandalphon help you.

Remember me introducing you to Archangel Sandalphon in Chapter 5? Well, his name roughly means "brother." However, I think it should mean "*big* brother," because this dude is *tall*! So tall that he is said to have his feet on Mother Earth and his head in Heaven. He is the emissary for prayers, and he lifts them from Earth and hands them to God. He is one of two humans whom God is said to have elevated to archangel status. (His human name in the Bible was Elijah.)

So if you've got an archangel just standing around waiting to help you with your prayers, why not let him?

5. Pray regularly.

I don't include this step as some sort of way of saying that if you don't pray often, God won't answer your prayers. I don't like that sentiment, because it puts God right back into a box and God doesn't fit in a box. But prayer *does* give you confidence.

It's like anything that you practice—you're just going to have more faith in your ability to do it successfully. So it's fine if your prayers for a given day are just: "Thank You, God, for giving me an awesome day, and amen." The more you pray, the more you'll hone your skills to see the answers that God is sending.

And God *is* sending them.

THE MAGICAL POWER OF SILLY

I'm a fully self-aware, open, out-of-the-closet . . . silly person. Nearly every close friend I have has some measure of silly in them. My sister and her husband are afflicted with silly. My nephew and nieces come by their silliness completely honestly.

I also have to confess that I'm probably a silliness carrier. The most serious of people, if they spend any time with me at all, start showing signs of silly-itis within a very short time. If you listen to my radio show or attend one of my lectures and you don't have any silly in you, then I must warn you that you're at risk for exposure to hopelessly silly shenanigans coming into your life. (So don't say I didn't warn you!)

I hardly think I need to tell you this, but things in the world are *extremely* heavy right now. I mean, really . . . it's just too much, don't you think? I'm serious when I tell you that I feel as though the number one thing I do on social media these days is hide political posts. I just can't take the energy of it all. It seems to me that the energetic weight on the shoulders of so very many countries around the world right now is overwhelming. The burdens . . . stress . . . fear . . . It's crushing the joyful spirit of many people.

The problem with that energy is that it suppresses our ability to manifest the things we truly want. When our thoughts are so turned toward worry and fear for the future, we're not in a place of creating much in the way of happiness. But there are antidotes to the negativity. There are ways to push back the worry and bring back in the lighthearted joy in our lives that we're Divinely due.

Meditation is a good antidote. So is exercise. But I think one of the most powerful ways to push the gray away and bring in the sparkly light of laugher is silliness.

So I'm just going to go right out on a limb here and proclaim myself a silly expert! If you find yourself in a situation where you need to rehab from seriousness, I've got you covered. Here are some of the ways I can recommend that you bring more silly into your life:

- First of all, I really think silly works best when you're practicing it with someone else. I mean, you can be silly by yourself, but somehow it lacks some of the oomph of doing it with a friend. Find yourself a silliness partner and start acting all willy-nilly!

- If you have a young child in your life, they're *true* experts at silly. Sit down with them and let them guide you in the world of joyful frivolity.

- Dogs are also happy to go on a nonsensical journey with you. (At least, mine are.) Just get down on the floor and roll around, play with them, and make funny noises.

- One of the things I do is to text something silly to my best friends. At least one of them will jump in with both feet and join in! All of them will if they aren't busy with something else.

Find the funny in everything you can. And then laugh and laugh and laugh!

I'm sure you can think of your own ways to bring up your inner silly child. Use it to push out the worry and bring back your joy!

FOLLOW YOUR HEART (MOST OF THE TIME)

Mind versus heart. It's a conflict as old as humanity. Do you listen to the intellectual advice of your noggin, or do you follow the pining of your heart?

We in the spiritual community have a tendency to say, "always follow your heart," but sometimes it's not that easy. And while I generally tend to agree with that point of view, I don't know that it's *always* the right path.

Part of the problem lies in the perception that following your heart has been a mistake. You fall in love with Sam or Sue or take a big risk to chase a dream, and things don't go quite the way you expected. You stop trusting yourself, and when you stop trusting yourself, your ego *really* kicks in and takes advantage of that. This is what gets you into that heart-versus-mind dilemma.

People tend to think of their minds as being separate from their hearts, even from their spirits. How many times have you found yourself saying, "Oh, my head tells me to do *this*, but my heart tells me to do *that*"? As if your head and your heart were that metaphorical angel on one shoulder and devil on the other.

More often than not, you may think of your heart as being the angel and your mind as being the devil. This is a bit unfair to your mind. In its own way, your mind is only trying to help you and protect you.

Our minds aren't big into risk. Our hearts are more willing to say, *Ah, just go for it!* Especially if the question at hand is romantic in nature.

Is there anything in life that offers us a greater high or a bigger crash than love? And as we consider this the domain of the heart, we tend to give in. I'm not saying that there's anything wrong with that.

However . . .

Do you, a friend, or a family member have a tendency to get stuck in a pattern or unhealthy cycle? A repeated routine when it comes to love? Ever known someone who just keeps attracting the same kind of partner over and over again? Usually when that happens, it's not a good thing. And when your friend has fallen for someone who treats them badly (for the fourth time!), wouldn't you tell your friend it's time to listen to reason before doing it again?

This involves being aware of the pattern. And the mind is the analytical expert in your metaphorical consulting group. And still the heart is beating fast and saying, *Oh, just go for it!* So let's talk about what to do when your heart says, *Go left,* but your mind says, *Oh, heck no. Go right.*

First of all, let your mind have its say. Trust me on this. It's going to anyway. It will invade your sleeping dreams or just hover over you like a cloak of anxiety. It's not going to go away. And you shouldn't want it to. It might have a point, you know. So do yourself a favor and give it the floor.

What does that mean, you ask?

Do this: Find some quiet time alone. Put on your very best objective-listener hat and grab some paper and a pen. Now, write down everything your head has to say about the decision you're trying to make. Don't argue with your head. Just write it all down. If you let your mind say its piece, then usually it will quiet down.

Once you've got it all down on paper, there are some things you should look for.

- First of all, are you experiencing déjà vu here?

- Are you seeing a pattern in your behavior that you need to address?

- Let's just keep our love life example going here. Are the reasons not to proceed in a relationship with your new heartthrob the same reasons you left the last two romances? (Because if they are, then your mind is trying to say, *"Puh-lease*, can we *not* do this *again*?")

- Does the choice that your heart wants you to make feel to you as though it's out of integrity?

- Do you have a sense that the path you're about to head down feels morally wrong to you?

- Are you going to like yourself in the morning?

Look at every item on the list that your mind gave you for following its lead. How do you feel about each one? Is it logical? Or does it feel to you like it's fear based?

Because living your life through fear is simply no way to go.

Okay. So now it's time to let your heart back in. If your mind starts to act up, just say aloud: "Dear mind, thank you so very much for all your advice. I greatly appreciate your desire to help me and to keep me safe. I promise to consider your point of view. But now I need you to be quiet and allow me to sort out my feelings."

I know it seems silly, but seriously, I've found that letting my mind have its say, thanking it, and then asking it for a moment alone with my heart really does work!

If your heart is asking you to follow a well-worn path back through the same forest that you keep getting lost in, then I would highly suggest you reconsider. However, if you can look at your mind's list of arguments and truly, objectively tick them off as fear based or out of alignment with you experiencing life to its fullest, then follow your heart. Chances are, your heart is going to win.

But let's not tell your mind that.

WISHING AWAY TIME

I don't know about you, but I feel as though time just continues to pick up momentum. As I'm writing this chapter, it seems as if I was shoveling snow two months ago, yet somehow we're in the last few weeks of summer, with autumn turning her beautiful gaze our way. I got home from teaching a two-day course in July, went to the grocery store, picked up the dry cleaning, blinked, and suddenly it's August!

I used to think that this phenomenon was an aspect of getting older. But it doesn't matter whom I bring this seemingly whirlwind-year concept up to, young or old; they're all in agreement that time is flying by faster and faster. And with that comes increased stress to get everything done. Most of us work in a world with deadlines.

Speaking of which . . . why do we call them *"dead*lines"? What a terrible word! Couldn't we call them *"life*lines"? Because, really, they're just dates to help us get the most out of life? Maybe sports enthusiasts would prefer *goal* lines!

Nevertheless, my life is full of them in some form. Book deadlines. Card-deck deadlines. Magazine-article deadlines. My electronic calendar is awash with them. And therein lies part of what is accelerating time: our desire to accelerate how much we accomplish. Not just in a given year, but in a lifetime. We're slaves to society's definition of success. So much to do, but not enough time to do it in. Often we just act, and hope for the best. Maybe we should have thought things through a bit more—but who has the time for that?

Well, frankly . . . we should. I have a dear friend who would say she felt like a slave to "the tyranny of the urgent." What she meant was that there were so many urgent matters to attend to that she never had time to focus on the big picture. And when we don't focus on where we want to go, we often wind up someplace that's less than satisfying.

So many of us are severely under-vacationed. We need a rest. We need time to think. Time to slow our gallop toward the finish line, not only so that we don't miss out on the joys of life, but also so that we don't forget ourselves and not win the race we meant to participate in. We might win someone else's idea of the right race, but not ours.

A lot of people are saying that 55 is the new 40. As time flies by, we've moved what we consider to be "middle age" to higher and higher numbers. I clearly remember growing up thinking that 55 was ancient, while I now think it's an age where things are just getting started! Still, as I get older, I also feel this sense of time encroaching upon my goals and that if I'm going to get everything done that I want in this lifetime, I had better step up the pace. But stepping up the pace is part of what makes time go faster, so isn't that counterproductive?

I'm very careful about not "wishing away" time. Ever catch yourself saying, "I can't wait until spring"? Or, "I can't wait until vacation"? Or the holidays, graduation, retirement . . . You name it. This is wishing away time. When your focus is on a future date, you're not living in the "now." Having your attention on what is to come may seem to make time stand still, but my experience is the opposite. When the anticipated date finally rolls around, I always look back and think, *Where did the time go?* And we all experience vacations going by in the blink of an eye. Once you've wished time to move fast, it's tricky magic to wish it back to going slow for any given week, because your Genie is running on high momentum.

You may have noticed by the Genie Academy lessons that I'm a big proponent of lists. I have them everywhere and usually rewrite them at least once a week. Making lists helps me stay focused. It keeps me thinking about what really matters and allows me a little freedom from the tyranny of the urgent in order to focus upon the fulfillment of the rewarding. I also believe it keeps time from just slipping through my fingers.

Another method I use to keep time under control is to allow for magical moments every day. Look for and embrace those poignant, awe-filled, or hilarious experiences—and then hold on to them. Even if it's just for a few minutes. It's a great way to learn how to use your magic to manipulate your personal experience of time.

Find time to think. Find time to take quiet walks. Make lists. Review your goals. Make sure you're headed where you really, truly want to go.

And, most importantly, be in the now.

* *

GENIE ACADEMY

Lesson #10: Daily Magic Reminders

So many things can distract us from our daily magic practices that I like to hide little reminders in my day. For example, I have my daily prayer song in most of my music playlists. If I've already prayed that day, I just skip over it. However, at least once or twice a week, the song will start to play and I'll realize, *Oops!* I'll stop what I'm doing to get my daily magical prayers taken care of.

Another magical reminder is to put notes in your calendar. Set an alarm every day that pops up on your smart device or computer that says, "Ask your angels for help!" or "Make a wish!"

You can also leave handwritten notes or cards around your home, car, workplace, or anywhere you'll see them often.

Come up with some fun ways to remind yourself every day to stay awake, pray, be silly, follow your heart, stay in the now—and just have a magical life!

* *

CHAPTER 7

$\mathcal{L}$IFE $\mathcal{M}$AGIC

Now that we've covered the aspects of daily magic, let's talk about the broader topic of life magic. There's a famous saying that goes, "There are only two ways to live your life. One is as though nothing is a miracle. The other is as though everything is a miracle."

As we just explored, *daily magic* consists of the things that a good Genie does every day. However, *life magic* is more of an overall philosophy. It may not require a specific action from you seven days a week, but it should always be in the back of your mind. Life magic is the big picture of what you believe, how you act, and the way you live your life. It's living life *knowing* that everything is a miracle.

SHOW ME YOUR DIAMOND

This planet has some amazing souls living on it. Deeply caring, openhearted people who live lives of service to others. The ones they're devoted to might be family, children, friends, or total strangers needing a helping hand. These people are deserving of our utmost gratitude and compassion.

Well, maybe.

I know I probably just shocked you with that line. But this section is about making yourself a priority without feeling guilty, so in a moment we're going to be breaking down that opening statement.

I have a friend who is the ultimate caretaker. It doesn't matter if it's her husband or her kids, friends in need, or even someone she just met, she's likely to sideline her hopes and dreams in order to fulfill other people's requests from her. I know that when she does manage to do something for herself that necessitates her not doing something for someone she cares about, she struggles with the guilt the entire time. She is one of the most talented and deserving people I know, and yet she is constantly setting aside what she wants from life in order to make others happy. Because of this, she is the inspiration for this section of the book, which is about the need for staying in balance with your life magic.

So here are my 10 points to ponder in order to dissuade you from feeling guilty about being your own number one priority:

- **Everyone on Earth is equally important.** We're all of equal value. No one stands above. It is possible to perceive that someone is more important due to the position they hold in their career or how well known they are. But that's just an illusion. It isn't true. And it isn't true *because* . . .

- **We're a beautiful mosaic.** A cosmic quilt. Each of us is a piece of a Heavenly puzzle that creates the most dazzling of pictures . . . but only if every piece is in place. Otherwise, there's a hole. And I don't care how gorgeous any completed puzzle is, your eye will always go to the missing puzzle piece if they're not all there. Right?

- **If the puzzle is incomplete, and its beauty is so greatly diminished by any missing piece, then we** *need* **every piece in order to be whole.** (Which just brings us right back to Point #1: that all the pieces are of equal importance.)

- **Everyone's life purpose is important.** You have dreams for yourself, and you have them for a reason. That reason is *not* so that you can spend your life pining away for that which you always wanted but which will never be. Think of your life purpose and dreams as a beautiful, perfect diamond the size of your hand. Now, I don't know about you, but I'd love to see that diamond! The whole world would love to see that diamond! Diamonds are famed for reflecting light in a dazzling way that will quite literally put stars in the eyes of all who gaze upon it.

  We *need* to see that diamond! But if you put that diamond in a trunk somewhere so that you can busy yourself polishing everyone else's diamonds, then we're all diminished. The light in the world is less. Our puzzle is incomplete. We as a world full of souls are all not quite what we could have been.

- **Deeply caring, openhearted people who live lives of service to others are deserving of our utmost gratitude and compassion—if and only if their life purpose is service.** Here, we're amending the lines that began this section because that statement is true if, and only *if*, that is their diamond. If in dedicating their lives to others, they experience great joy and fulfillment because that's their life purpose, then yes—we owe them everything!

  If it is not their diamond, then they're creating a sacrifice, however well-intentioned, that isn't in their highest, greatest good and therefore is not in the highest, greatest good of the world.

  Now, I just want to say, for 100 percent clarity, that I'm absolutely *not* saying that we shouldn't look out for others, care for those we love, or give to those in need. (Please don't write me angry letters on that point.) What I *am* saying is that if your entire life is spent making other people's needs more important than your own to the point that yours never get seen to, then you're not just hurting yourself—you're hurting all of us.

If your life purpose is solely service to others or helping others to fulfill their life purpose, then that's awesome! You aren't sacrificing anything, because that's what brings you joy. You've got your diamond out and your puzzle piece is in place and all is well. If that life leaves you unfulfilled and doesn't give you joy, then I suggest you reconsider whether it really *is* your life purpose.

- **You can be a role model to others.** Consider what you are teaching your children. If your diamond is in a trunk somewhere and your puzzle piece is completely missing, what does that say? Does it speak a message of compassion? Or does it say, "Hey, watch me. Throw your diamond into that trunk over there and grab a cloth. We'll go polish other people's diamonds"?

- **Not making yourself a priority, not focusing on making your dreams come true, is most likely coming from a lack of self-love.** In short, caring for others doesn't work nearly as well if you don't care for yourself, too. Self-love is critical. It is the magnifying glass through which we can focus love to others. If we're empty, then we have nothing to give to those around us.

- **Making sure your needs and priorities are met is not selfish.** It's healthy. Yes, there are selfish people in the world who only care for themselves, not anyone else. That's not what I'm saying you should do. Of course you should care for others. And I assure you those selfish people aren't on their life purpose. There's no way that their life purpose is to walk all over everyone else to get what they want.

Their puzzle piece is missing, and their diamond is probably in a vault somewhere because they're living in the irrational fear that someone will take it.

- **You are magic.** You have an inner Genie! You're an amazing, fabulous, incredible child of the Divine. There's nothing stopping you from seeing to those you love, being kind to others, while still making sure that *you* have the life of your dreams. You may not be priority number one on your list every single moment of every single day, but when you look at the big picture over time, when you really perceive what is happening as a whole, you should be sitting at the top most of the time.

- **A world where we're all making our life purposes come true is possible.** Imagine a world where our Divine light shines bright. A world where we teach our children that, yes, they have a magical, amazing reason for being here and they should pursue that and not let anything stand in their way. Envision a world where our spouses completely support us going after our dreams and, in return, we support them, and we support our friends and even strangers. All the diamonds are out, and it's spectacularly bright in the world. All the puzzle pieces are present, and the picture is breathtaking!

That's why you should be number one on your priority list. *That's* why you should never, ever feel guilty about it. We need you on your life purpose. We need your diamond out and shining so that the world is so full of light that darkness can't and won't prevail.

We need your piece of the puzzle or none of us are whole.

So no guilt. No sacrifice. No self-judging.

Love yourself. Show your light. Be your number one.

FIND YOUR FAMILY

Family is important to having a magical life. When most people think of family, they first turn their attention toward what we call their "family of origin." It's those folks with whom they share biological or adoptive bonds, including moms, dads, siblings, grandparents, cousins, aunts, and uncles. In other words, it's that very traditional definition of the word *family.*

Unfortunately, birth families don't always turn out the way we'd hoped. Parents pass away; siblings become estranged. Maybe you're just *so* different from the rest of your family that there's a lack of understanding and compassion for your point of view. That can create a situation where you might feel lonely or without support. You might experience a sense of loss or emptiness if your family of origin is either missing or not functioning well. If that's you, then as a Genie who wants you to be happy, supported, and completely fulfilled, I have news for you.

There's another kind of family. It's called a "family of choice." In fact, you may very well have a family of choice; you've just never used that term before.

A family of choice is composed of people that come into our lives without any sort of biological connection. Usually they're folks we might traditionally call friends. But as time goes by, they become more. They become more because they're with us for everything important. They're there for joy and for loss. They share holidays with us, but they also share our heartbreak when things go wrong. Sometimes they're replacements for birth families due to distance or estrangement, or frankly just because we feel a lack of respect from the family we were born into. Our families of choice fill in the empty spaces for us. They love us. They're loyal to us. They make us feel whole.

When you feel loved and respected and cared for, then you can more easily connect with your Genie within and manifest other magical things in your life.

Look around you. Who in your life might actually fall into the category of family of choice? Who is there for you? Who can you trust your secrets to? Who loves you no matter what? Who revels in the fact that you're weird? Well, maybe I shouldn't assume you think you're weird. Personally, I think I'm very weird and I love it! But either way, you know what I mean.

Some famous TV and movie examples of what I would call families of choice include Carrie, Samantha, Charlotte, and Miranda on *Sex and the City*; the entire cast of *Friends*; those eccentric scientists on *The Big Bang Theory*; the crew of *Star Trek*; and Harry Potter and those kid wizards at Hogwarts. Heck, I'd even say a little band of wacky colleagues stuck on an island together after a three-hour tour would count. (But I suppose I'm dating myself by bringing up *Gilligan's Island*, aren't I?)

I'm very blessed, as I have both a happy family of origin and a happy family of choice. When I moved to the Midwest from the town I was born in, nearly 20 years ago, I left behind my ability to see my family of origin on a daily basis. I distinctly remember sitting down on the stairs of my new home and starting to cry because I missed my sister after only three days in my new town. Of course, we still talked regularly, and nowadays there's that whole texting thing, which is alternately a blessing and a curse depending on what else is going on. But still, we all need someone to physically be with. Someone to be close to. And so while I'd never really heard the term *family of choice*, I still found myself seeking one out.

When I made my big cross-country move, I was hardly the only person heading west. It was a boom time for that part of the country. I found it hard to meet people, but when I did, I was always hoping that they had a lot of friends. It was so funny because it invariably turned out that they were hoping the same about me! It felt as if we were a city of strangers.

Eventually, I met three guys who would become my family of choice. (I mentioned them in Chapter 4—they're my like-minded Genie-ology group.) They were all relatively new to the state, having moved here from various parts of the country. We started hanging out. We started traveling around the world. Whenever it was possible, we were together. In time, we became conscious of what was happening. We started to realize that this was more than a group of friends; it was a family.

Now for us, this was a real milestone in our relationships. Like I said, many people have what an outsider might peg as a family of choice without noticing it. And that's certainly fine. But once we really became aware of our bond, we chose to name it—to call it *family*. It was our way of honoring what we had created, as well as sort of cementing it into place. And that's when we stopped being friends and started being brothers.

Our family has grown, as families tend to do. All of my brothers got married. One of my brothers now has a six-year-old son. So I have family-of-choice in-laws and a family-of-choice nephew!

Somewhere during that time, as everyone started to marry and careers became more all-encompassing, we began to struggle to find time to see one another. This distressed us, so we had to institute a mandatory lunch every month. It's always the same day of the month. It doesn't work perfectly because my brothers all have big careers and I'm often on the road. But we still do a pretty good job getting at least three of the four of us together at any given time.

I'm sharing this with you so that you'll be aware that families of choice require work and care, the same as any relationships. You may have chosen these people, but that doesn't mean you can't drift apart if you don't keep an eye on things. You might even want to ask yourself if your family of choice could use some special attention right now.

Respect, appreciation, kindness, and love are critical, whether your primary family is one of birth or one of choice. If you're lucky, then that works out with your family of origin. But if for any reason your family of origin isn't exactly giving you what you need and deserve, the point of this section on life magic is to let you know that you have another option.

BE THE TRUE, AUTHENTIC YOU—ALWAYS!

Perhaps I *was* born all sparkles and rainbows. I'd like to believe that we all are! But when I was a child, those traits got thrown under dark clouds. Those clouds had three names: *abusive father, unforgiving and judgmental religion,* and *mean kids in school.* By the time I was five, I was no longer looking up, but looking down—literally.

Everywhere I walked, I stared at the pavement. I didn't smile at people unless my mother asked me to. I certainly didn't look others in the eye. All I expected to receive were disapproving looks and defamatory labels, so I went inward.

Now, I know that a little Radleigh under dark clouds is probably not what you envisioned. People who know me or hear me speak are always shocked by that, yet we all have our stories. We've all had euphoria, and we've all had tragedy. I hope by explaining to you how I went from a terrified little kid to a joyful believer in life, you'll understand the importance of self-love and accepting your authentic self.

So, what brought me back out into the sunlight? How did I get my smile back? The answer to that also has three aspects:

- The love and wisdom of a dedicated mother

- Faith in the Divine

- Finding the courage to be fully myself, without regard to anyone else's opinions

It only takes a moment's contemplation to realize that each of these three things is the magical antidote to the three things that put me under a cloud in the first place.

1. The first thing that helped me was the love and wisdom of a dedicated mother. In your own life, this kind of devotion may not come from your mom. It can come from your dad, a grandparent, a sibling, or even a beloved friend or teacher. The most important thing to keep in mind is that somewhere in your life, there's *someone* loving you. There's someone who is trying to get you to see that you're amazing. In my case, it was my mom, and yes, she was there all along, trying to convince me I was quite fabulous. The problem was that when I was a child, her voice was drowned out by the chorus of others. And even as a child, I found it easy to dismiss my mom's opinion as not objective. I was her kid, after all.

But in time, as I grew up, those messages from my mother were like seeds planted deep in my heart. They lay dormant until such time as I was willing to come out into the sun. And then those words of wisdom grew, took root, and bloomed into affirmations I could assimilate into my identity. The voices of negativity from others seemed petty and unimportant in comparison to the words of love and compassion from my mom.

Take my message to heart: Life is magic. Love and compassion will always win over pettiness and unkindness. It might take a little time, but love will always win.

2. Next, I'd like to address my deep faith in the Divine. The fear of a judging and angry God within the religion I experienced as a child wound up having the most magical, amazing, and beautiful result. It drove me headlong into the arms of a loving, adoring, and uplifting God within my own personal spirituality!

Like a little lost child, I went seeking and there waiting for me was pure and unconditional love. The Divine just couldn't wait to lift me up, hold me tight, and show me the rainbows that were appearing as the clouds broke apart and the sunshine shone on my face. The Universe loved me beyond reason or understanding. And the knowledge of that lit me up from within. How could I possibly continue to look down at the pavement when there was so much beauty to see all around me beaming down from above?

3. Once I understood the guidance my mother instilled in me and had faith that Heaven loved me, it wasn't very hard to stop caring what other people thought. I stopped hiding. I became more and more the *true* me. I started smiling at everyone! If I had a compliment to offer to a total stranger, I offered it. I gave my suits to charity and bought clothes with sparkles on them. My boring shoes gave way to those with Swarovski crystals as I began to wear on the outside the sparkles I felt on the inside.

This is when *everything* changed for me! This is when I discovered my own Genie within. I realized that the things that I had been taught to dim down or to self-loathe were the very things that when brought out into the sun created pure magic. In retrospect, I had been using the magic all along, but to hold myself in a life I didn't want. When I started fully loving myself, being the completely authentic me, and following my Divine guidance, I was able to leave the corporate world of accounting and make my dream of being a spiritual teacher and author come true.

There's nothing here that isn't available to you. You can look around and find that person who loves you and is trying to instill self-love in you. You can make yourself listen to them and accept the truth of the message. You can open your heart to the love of the Divine and put your faith in its unending, unquenchable desire that you find joy and happiness. You can disregard the unkindness and judgments of others in favor of becoming more and more fully *you*.

Be the *you* that you were born to be. The *you* that the world needs. The *you* that can lead you right to your most blessed and Divine life purpose.

No Time Traveling

Ever catch yourself saying, "I just wish I could go back in time and change that *one* thing. It would make all the difference in the world"?

Maybe it might. For a long time, I wished I could go back in time and somehow change the things that put me under a cloud and made me terribly unhappy as a child and young adult. But here's the funny thing about time travel: you never know what might ripple forward. Every one of the things that I talked about in the previous section had a hand in making me who I am today. And who I am today is exactly who I want to be!

I'm now doing exactly what I want to be doing with my life. Yes, there are other things I'm currently wishing up for myself that haven't manifested just yet, but I keep getting peeks that they're headed my way. If I could go back in time and change this or that, I might just change something that would take away the joy and magic I'm experiencing in my life right now.

No, thank you!

What successful Genies do is have faith that the challenging experiences in the past were designed by Heaven to set them up to start making their life be what they want it to be right now. Today! Look at those past difficulties as metaphorical trips to the gym that have made you stronger and more capable to take on any dream and make it a reality.

Make Your Space Magical

When you really start to allow magic into your life, life will show you amazing new ways to bring more magic in. Over the years, I have come to include feng shui as a very important part of empowering your inner Genie to help you manifest the desires of your heart.

I didn't always know very much about this ancient art, but in 2007, I moved into a new home. In this neighborhood, almost everyone's garages opened up to an alley facing a row of garages belonging to the houses on the next street over. In one of those magical, synchronistic events that Genies get to experience, my garage opened up across the alley from the garage of a feng shui expert named Tanya Jahnke.

If you're not familiar with feng shui, it's all about creating a harmonious environment within your home, your office, or any other space. Feng shui considers your home to be a direct reflection of your life. Therefore, by making changes to your home and the placement of items in your outer world, feng shui seeks to bring balance and harmony to your *inner* world.

Practicing feng shui is a bit like releasing the Genie energy of your "lamp" out where it can help you to make magic. By exploring your house through the lens of feng shui, an expert like Tanya can uncover your blocks, identify patterns and symbols that are keeping you anchored in the past, and create a space that reflects your authentic self.

Some people are under the false impression that feng shui is only about decluttering your house, changing the colors of your walls, or moving furniture around. But it's actually so much more than that! It's a proven art that is 4,000 years old, used in nearly every culture in the world, in one form or another.

Feng shui can also be a very powerful tool in your inner Genie's manifestation toolbox. Think of it as a 3-D vision board for your life that can create opportunities, increase abundance, attract love, improve your health, increase joy, and manifest infinite blessings on every level.

When I first started bringing feng shui into my home, the results were nothing short of miraculous! Unexpected windfalls of abundance began to be showered on me, as well as other career opportunities that I hadn't imagined could present themselves so quickly.

As you know, I'm an intuitive, but my gift is not clairvoyance (the gift of seeing). I have claircognizance (the gift of knowing), with a little bit of clairaudience (the gift of hearing) thrown in. And yet, even though I'm not clairvoyant, when Tanya comes to clear our home, I can literally *see* the energy inside the house shimmering. Beyond that, the house feels like it's full of Divine light.

Tanya explained her philosophy to me: "Feng shui allows you to shift the energy in your home and life, release blocks and limiting beliefs, transform outcomes, and create infinite possibilities and opportunities. You can navigate the path of your life with intention and use feng shui as a powerful tool to positively influence every area of your life.

"Look at your home with fresh 'feng shui eyes.' What story is your house telling? What impressions would a stranger have if they were visiting your house for the first time? Are your passions, dreams, positive memories, and adventures on display? Are you holding on to items that you don't love, use, or need? Infuse your home with reminders of your true Self and create space for your dream life to take root."

I consider it a very important part of life magic to make sure that the place you live is an energetic match to the dreams you're trying to manifest. Feng shui can do that by bringing peace and harmony into your space, therefore making your life more magical.

At the end of this chapter, I'll share with you some things you can do to bring in increased abundance and opportunities that I have found work . . . *like magic!*

RANDOM ACTS OF MAGIC

There's an old parable that includes the line, "The good you do comes back to you." I couldn't agree more with that sentiment! It can be so easy to totally change someone's life with a simple kindness. Someone who is currently in a downward spiral of negative thoughts or emotions can suddenly have that momentum stopped or even reversed when you do a magical good deed for them. I call these "random acts of magic."

When it comes to doing a magical kindness, I follow my intuition. I may be touched by a story someone tells me on my call-in radio show that compels me to take action. Sometimes I may even hear my angels saying, "Help that person!"

That help might come in the form of a gift I send to them or by adding them to my personal prayer list. I always have a few $5 bills in my car to hand out to those in need when my angels tell me to. For example, I've helped pay for groceries for people ahead of me in line who didn't quite have enough money.

Whether you help someone financially or offer your time to a charity or worthy cause, you're telling the Universe (and yourself) that you realize that there's more than enough magic to go around for everyone, which in turn increases your confidence that the magic will be there for *you* when you need it.

MAKE FRIENDS WITH YOUR BODY

We're constantly bombarded with unattainable (or at least unsustainable) images of male and female beauty. Once again, this is where the comparison game turns into a trap.

Your body is constantly taking care of you. Your beautiful, magical soul is taking a ride in your physical self, and it deserves your gratitude and your love. Be kind to it when you look in the mirror or when choosing what food and substances to put into it.

"Happiness shortcuts," like sugar, alcohol, and drugs, are more often than not actually dead ends. It is not my intention here to tell you which things are healthy, okay, or detrimental to your health. Again, I believe that's a very personal thing that varies with each individual. I personally believe that Girl Scout Thin Mint cookies should be a controlled substance requiring a pre-scription and follow-up psychological care—that's how much I love them! I also know that I can't have too many of them in my home because I will binge, binge, *binge*.

Your body will tell you what is good and not good for you. Your intuition will provide you with guidance. Right here and right now you *know* in your heart what parts of your health need attending to and in what way. That might be "Get exercise" or "Become a vegan."

Remember: The Divine is not being mean to you by saying you need to go to the gym or remove certain things from your diet. What it *is* trying to do is make you an energetic match to your dreams so that you can access your Genie magic and fully use it to make your wishes come true.

Make friends with your body. Give it the care and compassion it deserves, and it will be friends with you.

AND THEN THERE'S THIS STUFF

Here are a few other life magic strategies that I promise will make your life happier, more fulfilling, and of course . . . more magical!

- **Choose focus over obsessing.** There's a big difference between obsessing and focus. Being focused is uplifting and hopeful. Obsessing is worrisome and fearful and leads to unhappiness.

- **Don't miss out on life through impatience.** It's much like wishing away time. If your attention is constantly trained on what is to come, then you're not in the "now" and a lot of potential happiness is eluding you.

- **Be fearless.** Never stop taking risks. Don't be afraid to take a leap of faith. All of these things lead to a more magical life.

- **Never wish for bad things to happen to other people.** Trust me, the old saying "What goes around, comes around" is true. To wish unhappiness or misfortune on another is setting the magic in motion for challenging things to happen to you. So just don't do it.

- **Never do something that you personally believe is "wrong."** It might actually be a bad idea, or it may just feel like the wrong thing for you personally. If your personal guidance says, "Don't do this," then honor that. Whatever it is, it won't go well, and you'll put yourself back in the Genie lamp, so just don't do that, either.

- **Allow awe and wonder to be a part of your life.** Never stop letting yourself be amazed by how beautiful the world is. Go to places that make you happy as much as possible, and do everything you can to make where you are a happy place.

- **Let others love you in whatever way they can.** Not everyone can love as intensely as you, nor can you love as intensely as every other person on the planet. Accept what is possible and give as much as you can. It all balances out in the end.

$\mathcal{G}$ENIE $\mathcal{A}$CADEMY

Lesson #11: Gold-Rock Cure for Abundance

One of the wishes that Genies will want to grant themselves is that of a prosperous and abundant life. In feng shui, a "cure" is basically a way of doing a little magic to establish the right energy to attract whatever you're looking to bring into your life. I have personally used this cure at my home for over a year, and the results have been nothing short of astounding! Symbolically, what you are creating is a mountain of wealth.

To start, you'll need to acquire eight river rocks of varying sizes. (Eight is the number of abundance.) You don't necessarily have to get the rocks directly from a river yourself, but they must be smooth and round, with no sharp or pointy edges. You'll also need a can of gold spray paint, as gold, of course, is the color of wealth. Try to find a shiny, metallic gold rather than a flat, matte shade.

Spray the eight river rocks with the metallic gold paint. Once dry, stack them outside to the right of the front door (when facing your house). Place the larger rocks on the bottom and build a symbolic mountain of wealth. While you're doing so, set your wealth-related intention or speak a statement of abundance out loud.

Feng shui very much relies upon things being neat and tidy. It's important to regularly check on your stones to make sure they haven't gotten covered in dust or cobwebs. I usually bring them in and wash them, and then thoroughly sweep the area around the front door so that it's as clean as possible. Then I restack the stones with the intention that I have just reset my mountain of wealth for the next big inflow of abundance.

+ + +

Lesson #12: Nine-Red-Candles Cure for Fame

This is another "cure" for prosperity; however, it also attracts blessings such as job offers, opportunities for professional promotion such as radio or magazine interviews, increased self-confidence, and maybe even a publishing contract! It can be used for whatever attention you are seeking to be drawn to yourself so that you can make your dreams come true.

You'll need nine red candles. The candles can be any shade of red and any size (tea light or pillar). Place the nine candles in the Fame & Reputation area of your home or office. (The Fame & Reputation area is center rear of the inside of your home or office.)

Light each candle. Once they are all lit, visualize your desired outcome or simply visualize your self-esteem and reputation being illuminated. Then blow each candle out.

You can repeat this cure whenever you need a boost. Do it for nine days in a row if you have a specific goal related to being seen, receiving accolades, or improving your self-confidence.

✦ ✦ ✦

Lesson #13: Create Your Own
Random Act of Magic Moment

During your next prayer or meditation session, tell Heaven and your angels that you'd like to have the opportunity to provide a random act of magic for someone. Then, throughout your day, start scanning for opportunities. Chances to do a kindness for someone will show up all around you, but you will have to stay awake in order to notice them. Make note in your journal or on a piece of paper of the kindnesses you do for others.

What you will notice very quickly is that other people are providing you with your own random acts of magic! The more magic you provide to others, the more magic will come back around as Heaven's reward to you!

✦ ✦ ✦

Lesson #14: Interview Your Body

For this meditation, you'll need some paper and something to write with.

Find some quiet time when you can be alone without interruption. I love to do this meditation while pampering my body. If you have the option, turn this into a time of gratitude for your body by lighting some candles and getting into a lovely bath. You can also fill your meditation space with one of your favorite smells through incense or a special perfume. Remember to focus on the fact that you are doing this for your *body*, not your mind.

Once you're settled in either a space of meditation or your body pampering experience, then go within and ask: "Body, what could I do for you that would really be of assistance?"

Then ask: "Body, what changes to my diet or routine would you like me to make?"

Write down the answers that come to you. Try not to edit what you write or question the answers that come to you. Just take the words as they come. Carry on your conversation with your body until you feel that the exercise is complete, or you hear your body say thank you.

CHAPTER 8

THOSE PESKY OTHER GENIES

News flash for you: you're not the only Genie running around making magic. *Everyone* has an inner Genie. To truly have a magical life, you're going to have to figure out when working with other Genies is a good thing . . . and when it's a bad thing.

As your energy shifts to being more positive and more spiritual, magical new people will be drawn to you! On the flip side, you may realize that some of the ones who have been in your life for a long time no longer feel good to you. In fact, as the sparkle comes back into your eyes, you may suddenly be able to see very clearly that you're no longer able to tolerate negative people.

As I mentioned in the Genie-ology section of Chapter 4, one of the ways in which people can partner with other Genies with positive results is to work in small groups. If you're going to work in partnership with other Genies, there are a few things you might want to keep in mind . . .

DIVERSITY IS DELICIOUS

Partnership is a very broad term that can mean anything from our most romantic and intimate relationships to something as emotionally unconnected as contracting with someone to remodel the kitchen. Nevertheless, every connection we make with other people contains the potential to have a powerful effect on us— especially over time.

When I was still working as a certified public accountant, my favorite part of the job was my team. I know that when people hear "CPA," their first thought is "that guy who does your taxes," but there are all kinds of jobs in the profession. During the span of my accounting career, I did just about everything. However, as time went by, the primary aspect of my job became the management of people. I had a *lot* of people working for me, and I was very good at managing—especially the hiring part.

Of course, I had a certain advantage when finding just the right people. I'm psychic! So I knew who would work well with others and who wouldn't. I even had other department heads offering to pay me to hire their teams for them! I didn't have a big secret, though. The key to a great team, in my mind, is diversity.

I adore diversity. Whether in work or personal life, I consider the mixing of different sorts of people akin to making a magic potion using only the most wonderful of ingredients. I love that element of taking a group of diverse, differently skilled individuals and putting them together as a team, then seeing what they create. The result will *always* be infinitely better than what could ever be put together by a team of members who are completely similar in their training and perceptions—trust me!

So, naturally, I think one of the keys to a very successful Genie partnership is teaming up with others who are different from you. Yes, of course, it's important to have common goals and ethics. But think of what can be accomplished if one person is incredibly intelligent and experienced, another is creative and brimming over with fresh ideas, and another is from a different geographical place with a unique cultural perspective . . . it can be astonishing!

Your Reality Isn't the Only Reality

Having an open mind is another thing that's very important for successfully working with other Genies. It is a very human trait to believe that the world is seen and interpreted by everyone else the same way it is by you, but hear me when I tell you that this *simply isn't true*!

Sadly, the belief that there's only one way to see the world is the primary cause of wars, divisiveness, and conflict between people. Stop and think about this for a moment: Just like a snowflake, you're unique. There's simply no one else like you. How could there be? After all, no one else has your genes or grew up with your family dynamics. No one else had the exact experiences you did through your childhood, going to school, and heading out into the workforce. No one met, interacted with, and was influenced by the same people in the same ways as you. You see the world in your own unique way.

Society forgets that what might seem perfectly logical and obvious to one set of people is absolutely ridiculous, crazy, or indefensible to another set of humans. It is utterly natural and good for you to have your own opinions and thoughts about any topic at all. But if you can keep an open mind, knowing that others may see things differently and for perfectly legitimate reasons, you'll save yourself a lot of anxiety and conflict with other Genies.

Becoming Someone Else's Genie

Over the last few years, I've learned a good many things. For example, I discovered that if you roll up socks in a suitcase, they take up less space than if you lay them flat. I don't know why that is, but it appears to be true. I've found that the key to traveling from country to country without taking your entire wardrobe is that "monotones are your friends," so you can mix and match outfits. I've also learned that it isn't possible for me to have a magical life if the majority of my relationships are with people who are drowning in drama. This last little bit was a big revelation to me—and a big challenge! You see, I used to give my power away to others almost as a way of life.

One of the things I've noticed about life is that birds of a feather really do tend to flock together. Since you're reading my book, it's either because you're like me in certain ways or you need to hear the message I have to share, or both. So let's see if I'm right. I'm going to describe *you* right now. (I'm really describing the *old* me, but I'm betting this is going to sound really familiar.) Here goes . . .

- **You're very conflict averse.** What that means is that you can't stand conflict. You'll go along with all kinds of things you don't really want to do just to avoid upsetting someone else or having an unpleasant or adversarial conversation.

- **You're a caretaker.** You'll always see to the needs of everyone around you before you see to your own (so you rarely get around to yours). Once again, this is partly because you just want everyone to be happy, but it's also just in your nature to care for others. You'll even skip *being who you really are* if that isn't who the people you love want you to be.

- **You have a lot of people in your life who are takers but don't give back in equal measure.** Takers also tend to have a *lot* of drama in their lives. For some reason, one just seems to go with the other. Because of that, you wind up getting caught up in that swirl of drama and charged emotions, making you anxious and nervous when these people are around. Still, you let them stay because you love them or because you can't bear the conflict or discussion that would occur if you were to walk away.

So, how'd I do? Does that sound like you?

If you were to stop and really take the time to analyze your relationships, you might discover that quite a few of them make you feel unhappy or anxious at times, or in a state of continuous fear or worry. What's curious to me is that often these unhappy alliances tend to be quite old. A person may have been part of your life for over a decade, and you hold on to the relationship because you're too softhearted to go through the drama that comes with bringing the arrangement to a close. (Or, perhaps, you simply still care for the person.)

Trust me, I know how hard this is. I have firsthand experience removing those types of relationships from my life, and Heaven knows it's not easy. It can be very, very challenging. But let me tell you something. A relationship that's making you unhappy is not meant to continue. You're supposed to be a free and joyful person. Those who honor you and bring happiness into your life—*those* are the ones that you should hold on to and shower your Genie magic on. If a relationship makes you feel trapped or devalued, consider that a sign that it's time to move in a new direction. And that direction is as far away from emotional imprisonment and a lack of balance in give-and-take as you can get.

When you become entrapped in a bunch of high-drama relationships with people who only take but don't give back, then you become *their* Genie. You're spending your magic making *them* happy, not yourself. If there's an equal balance of give-and-take, then that's great! Share the magic! But if you're just having your energy drained every time you're with them, then you've basically been shoved back into your lamp metaphorically, and they've become its master.

My term for these people is *drama masters*. They've managed to get control of your Genie lamp, and with that they bring a bunch of drama into your life that you wouldn't have otherwise.

But how to get free—now that's the difficult part. How to remove the painful influence and entrapment of someone who, in your heart of hearts, you *know* needs to go?

BREAKING FREE

A few years ago, my perception of relationships began to change dramatically. I don't have all the reasons at my disposal, but I think I just started to get tired. I got tired of saying yes to everyone when I really wanted to say no. I got tired of drama in my life. But I think the thing I got tired of the most was not being my authentic, unique, quirky self. I got tired of tailoring who I was to suit who was in front of me at the moment. I wanted to be purely *me*.

Now this created a predicament. Let me tell you something important that you need to know: *People don't like it when you change*. Actually, let me qualify that by saying that your *real* friends won't mind. A truly loving and uplifting life partner won't mind. But the drama masters you've been tailoring your life to? They get really upset when you stop catering to their every whim. When you stop being who *they* think you should be and start being your own true self, they don't like that at all. They expect the Genie in the lamp to just keep giving the same way you always have.

So in order to break out of my cocoon—in order to really fly—I had to deal with those people. And lots of times that meant conflict. In almost every situation, it meant releasing those people from my life. I had to learn to say no when that was the right thing for me.

The thing that's very hard about this is that just because someone is a "drama" type of person, that doesn't mean that I didn't like or even love them. They can be amazing people. They're just . . . *exhausting*. They drain all your Genie magic and rarely give back in equal measure based on what they take.

Once I decided to start clearing the drama masters out of my life, I didn't do it in any particular order. I didn't set up a process or sort through the people I knew in an organized fashion. I just became conscious that my life needed cleaning up. So whenever someone would call me, I would check in with myself afterward. If I felt drained, I would stop and think, *Okay. Is this how I usually feel with this person?* And if the answer was mostly yes, I would decide then and there to just let that person go.

I didn't have a big conversation. I didn't make my own bunch of drama out of it. I just stopped calling the person. I stopped answering the phone when they would call. I asked Raguel, the archangel of relationships, to let that drama master just drift away. I asked Zadkiel, the archangel of memory, to let them forget me.

And let me tell you, this made an amazing change in my life! It was like a tremendous weight had been lifted from my shoulders. I was calmer. I was happier. I was more positive. And I had worlds more energy.

Of course, there are still drama masters in my life. After all, there are some people you just can't release. You may have parents, children, a spouse, or co-workers you have to deal with because you just really have no choice. The best you can do is to limit their impact. But if you scroll through your social-media feeds and your phone's contact list, I bet you can find a lot of drama masters you *do* have a choice whether to associate with.

Also, don't just assume that you have no choice in the matter. I once worked for someone who was unbelievably negative. Empress of the Drama Queens, for sure! You know what I did? I stopped attending her meetings, because that's when she was the most volatile. I avoided connecting with her whenever possible. So, really consider who is truly a "no choice" person.

Now that the majority of the drama masters are gone, I'm so much happier—and I desperately want the same thing for you! I want you to be free from the lamp and not be anyone else's Genie. I want you to have the opportunity to love yourself by discovering who you truly are outside the confines of the drama kings and queens of your life.

What that means is that you're going to have to learn to say no. You're going to have to start clearing house. You're going to have to learn that any conflict you experience due to this time of transition—this time of *blooming*—will be relatively short, and you'll see when you're done that every second was worth it.

You'll have to learn to stand up for what you believe in. You'll have to be willing to defend your own beliefs and follow the Divine guidance that you've been given. More than anything, you have to do whatever it takes to be who you truly are rather than the diluted you that's busy being who everyone wants you to be.

So I want you to repeat the following phrases:

"No."

"Oh, I'm so sorry, I just can't do that."

"I understand where you're coming from, but that just isn't in line with my own integrity, so I'm going to have to decline."

"I hope you'll understand, but what you're asking of me feels like the wrong thing for me right now."

And then one more time . . .

"No."

* *

$\mathcal{G}$ENIE $\mathcal{A}$CADEMY

Lesson #15: Drama-Master Release Exercise

Grab a piece of paper, a pen, and your address book and/or personal electronic device, such as your phone or laptop. Think about all the people you regularly interact with. Look over your phone's contact list, your address book, and your social-media feeds. Notice whether you feel positive or anxious when you read someone's name or think about them. Then write down the names of all the people to whom you have a negative reaction.

Next, look at each name and decide if you have a choice about whether you interact with them or not. Really think about it. Don't just assume you have no choice. Maybe you can at least limit your contact. If they're a "no choice" person, take them off your list.

For the people left on your list, seriously think about what they take from you and what they give back. How balanced are the scales? Why do you want them in your life? For anyone where you feel the negatives are balanced by the positives, mark them off your list.

The names left on your list are your drama masters. Time to let them go.

I would highly encourage you *not* to make a big dramatic experience out of releasing your drama masters. They'll just take it as their chance to play victim and throw guilt and all kinds of negativity your way. And isn't that why you're releasing them in the first place, to get away from that?

* *

$\mathcal{G}$ENIE $\mathcal{L}$OVE

It starts with a whisper. A smile. A sparkle in someone's eye. A bashful blush where you turn away, but then, because you really can't help yourself, you turn back for another look.

Your heart flutters. Your breath quickens, or maybe you realize you're actually *holding* your breath. You have goosebumps.

No, you don't have the flu. It's *love*!

All of these are your first signs . . . indicators of, *Wow, something very magical is about to happen.*

Not everyone considers romantic love an important part of having a magical life, but the majority of people do. It has been an essential part of my happiness—after all, my last name *is* Valentine—so the topic of Genie love was destined to be a part of this book.

Love comes into your life in many ways. Sometimes it quietly slips in. Other times, it can hit you like a ton of bricks. I seem to consistently have the "ton of bricks" experience; I've never had love just inch its way into my life. However, other people I know seem to follow the soft, slow, and cautious method. Whichever way it happens for you, you know the power of love. It's joy! If ever my little catchphrase of "life is magic" were true, it's certainly the case when it comes to falling in love. And when love enters your experience, you can be assured that you either consciously or unconsciously wished it into your life.

If you don't currently have romantic love in your life, I'm going to share ways to harness your inner Genie magic to bring it in! But first, let's define some terms so that we're all on the same page about the different types of Genie love.

Soul Mates and Twin Flames and Romances . . . Oh My!

When people talk about relationships, they often use terms interchangeably that aren't really the same. If you are seeking true love, what exactly does that look like to you? Are you looking for a *soul mate*? Are you especially courageous and searching for a *twin flame*? (If you're looking for that, be careful what you wish for! I'll explain why in just a moment.) Are you simply after a lovely *romance*?

These are all perfectly wonderful and lovely things to ask for, but they do have their differences. And some people don't want *any* of those things; they just want companionship, someone in their lives with whom to go on walks, share dinners, or catch a movie.

Whatever the relationship, we're drawn to people who can help us grow, learn, and evolve. Relationships are like the sand in the oyster. Just as an oyster uses that bit of sand to build a perfect pearl, the experience of a relationship can cause us to develop in beautiful ways. We're here on Earth to gain experience—to become more than we are. Although we might like things to be different, our growth seems to progress as much through challenge as through joy, both of which will be found to varying degrees in your romantic relationships.

Now, let's distinguish between the three main types of romantic relationships: soul mates, twin flames, and romances.

— **Soul mates** are a topic that people seem to talk about a lot, so it surprises me that there are so many misconceptions about what the term truly means. Many think of soul mates as being a romantic relationship with a person who's not just perfect for them but practically *designed* for them.

The only part of this concept that I actually agree with is the word *perfect*. And even then, people don't mean what *I* do when it comes to "perfect." In this context, I mean someone who's perfect at helping you *grow*. Someone who is perfect at helping you evolve and accomplish certain goals you had in mind when you agreed in Heaven to incarnate here on Earth. As such, that means this person is also perfect at pushing your buttons and making you utterly crazy!

A "perfect" soul mate is not someone who never, ever upsets you or makes you unhappy. That's not a man. That's a mannequin. (Or, I guess, a *woman*equin, depending on your interests.)

Here's the scoop—soul mates don't have to be romantic. Frankly, many—if not most—of the ones in your life won't be. Soul mates are simply *souls* with whom you agreed to come to Earth for very special reasons. You've likely incarnated together many, many times—and in my personal observation, you probably *have* had at least one romantic past life with them. (What I've noticed among my friends is that a soul-mate friendship seems to be less crazy-making than a soul-mate romance. So take that for what it's worth.)

When you think of your soul mate, you feel it in your heart. When you first meet or see them, you just *know*. Even if in this lifetime that soul mate is your platonic best friend, the relationship has a powerful energetic and emotional connection.

Naturally, it's nice when your romantic relationship has a soul-mate connection to it. It's why we crave it. In fact, as a society, we've sort of idolized this notion. And I think those relationships really are worthy of being cherished, so long as we really see them as they are: powerful connections designed to help us grow in ways that will touch us deeply. (And also drive us nuts!)

— A **twin-flame relationship** is an even *more* powerful connection than a soul mate. There's only one twin flame possible for you out there, and it's always romantic. You will know that you're with a twin flame when you find a person who instinctively knows everything there is to know about you on a spiritual and emotional level. Imagine the intensity! Imagine the euphoria!

And imagine the insane challenges and emotional upheaval that will come with the sheer bliss (because they *will* come in equal measure). In a twin-flame relationship, you're going to be pushed to grow and evolve in ways you can't imagine unless you've experienced it. Yes, the rewards are great! But the demands are even greater.

— Finally, I want to give some credit to just regular, lovely **romances**. Believe it or not, you don't have to be with a soul mate or a twin flame to be deliriously happy and loved and content in a relationship. When people ask me for a reading regarding relationships, 90 percent of the time they ask me about a soul mate. My response to them is always, "Does it have to be a soul mate? Can't we just ask Heaven when a joyful, supportive relationship that will make you incredibly happy will come into your life—and leave the labels to the Divine to sort out?"

Not surprisingly, they always say yes!

THE PERFECT IMPERFECTION

Like I said, people tell me all the time about their desire to find the "perfect person." It almost always causes me to raise an eyebrow while asking them what they mean by "perfect."

I believe that if what we imagine to be a perfect person walked into our lives, we'd be so bored out of our gourds that we'd dump them within a year. If our partners don't push our buttons and create for us the agitation necessary for garnering personal insights, then what good are they? On a spiritual level, we're always looking to grow and evolve, so we seek out friends and lovers who will help us with that objective.

If you look deep enough at relationships that have collapsed, very often you would discover that they ended because no one was learning anything anymore. So if by looking for the "perfect one," you mean someone imperfect enough to drive you slightly crazy, then I agree with your search. Imperfect is perfect. The perfect one is imperfect. And you have my blessing to proceed.

As to "the one"? I don't really buy that part, either. Souls incarnating here on Earth have evolved greatly from the way they were just 100 to 200 years ago. We're no longer marrying the only person we can find, growing barley, having kids to help out on the farm, and staying with one person our entire lives because we have no other options. My perception is that the souls that come into life now want 3 degrees, 4 careers, 28 different jobs, and 4 different partners during their time on the planet. What we're trying to get out of our lifetimes has accelerated and evolved so much that many of us feel we can't get everything we need in a lifetime from just one person.

In the grand scheme of things, love is infinite and love is eternal. However, sometimes the magic shared between two Genies fades. They've learned all they can in being together, and once that happens, they retreat to their respective Genie lamps. Life won't be much fun in there for long, so the time comes to move on.

Often, "the one" is really "the one to help us grow in the here and now." Sometimes, they're "the one who will be teaching us lessons for this moment of our lives."

Despite society's romanticizing of the notion of staying with one person for 75 years, there's nothing wrong with relationships evolving so that we have several in a lifetime. Maybe in looking for the perfect *one*, all we are doing is setting ourselves up for disappointment and failure.

The main thing I want to do here is to release you from a useless little emotion called fear. From my standpoint, it doesn't serve you to fear that you'll never find the "perfect/imperfect" romantic partner. I completely believe that the Universe abhors a vacuum. That's generally a scientific saying, but what I deem it to mean with regard to a romantic relationship is that if you have a place in your heart to give love, then the Universe won't waste that. In perfect timing, someone will come to receive that love. The tricky part is to make sure you wish for someone who will also give in equal measure back to you.

Now You See Me?

This brings me to the *way* in which most people want to be in love. What is it about the feeling of near intoxication that makes us so deliriously happy? Is it a chemical in our brains? Are we just so awash with hormones that we become addicted to the feeling? Or is it something more?

I have a theory. When we fall in love, we suddenly see the object of our affections as they truly are. Yes, yes . . . I know from a "real-world" standpoint, sometimes love can make us see people through rose-colored glasses. However, what if there's something more to it than that?

What if when we fall in love, there's a part of us that slips back over to the other side of the veil? What if falling in love opens our souls to the feelings we experience in Heaven? What if being in love is where we actually see someone (and perhaps ourselves) as the true souls that we really are? Could it be possible that this is the way we feel about everyone when we're no longer in physical bodies but prancing around the stars in our spiritual forms? Do we suddenly see the Divine light in all souls, thereby making us "in love" with everyone, once we're in Heaven?

Maybe when we stop feeling in love with someone, it's because we've relaxed back into the "real world" and our physical existence, and we start hiding. We start hiding our true selves from them, and they hide their true selves from us.

So to summarize . . . imperfect is perfect. It helps us grow, evolve, and learn to love more. Perfect would be imperfect even if it existed.

You have more than one chance at love. In fact, I'd say you have infinite chances. You have nothing to fear about the future and nothing to regret about the past.

Love yourself first. Clichéd, I know. But still the truest truth you're going to come across. When you love yourself, you give love to your partner in the purest way possible. You also command that same love back from them. You stop allowing yourself to be taken advantage of, and it's then that you can experience the love you've been dreaming of.

That perfect, imperfect love.

THAT'S GONNA LEAVE A MARK

Some people just leave a mark. I know, that's so "country-music-song-ish," but it's still true. Everyone has that one relationship that just really felt like *magic*. If that relationship dissolves for whatever reason, it can really be hard to get the magic back with someone else. There are several reasons for that.

First of all, the blending of Genie love between two people is always a unique concoction. No two people are alike, so no two blends of romance magic can ever be the same. It also creates challenges when people try to compare current romantic relationships with ones they've had in the past. As I've mentioned before, the comparison game is a trap. It's easy to view the past through rose-colored glasses because we've forgotten the difficulties that caused the previous relationship to end.

When any relationship ends, it's important to try to be grateful for what the other person pointed out in you that you cherish and what you learned about what you need in a relationship. The people who leave the most indelible impressions upon you are those who taught you something magical about yourself. If you've been blessed to have experienced such a relationship and because of it you're obsessed with looking backward, I have some magical advice I'd like to give you.

The mistake you might be making is that you give the credit for the magic to the other Genie in the relationship. You're forgetting that the magic you experienced wasn't the other person; it was within *yourself*. It was something that the other person awakened in your heart. It's important for you to remember that *you* carry that magic inside you, and no one can take it away from you.

In other words, your ex is not the only person you can create magic with. Don't give your ex all the credit for the magic you felt. Give them the credit for being the right canvas for you to paint that side of yourself and bring it out so you could see it. They deserve that. But your ex is not the source of the magic within you that you wish to experience more of. Whoever they are, your ex was in your life for a reason. They're also now *out* of your life for a reason.

SPEAKING OF EXES

I'm amazed by the number of people who ask me for readings about whether their ex is going to come back into their romantic life. This desire is so much more common than you may realize. Part of the reason why I hear the question so often may be because the spiritual communities I teach in are full of good and kind people. Once the exes are gone, these deeply spiritual people with soft hearts forget the bad and start remembering only the good. It's an endearing trait, but it's also a trap because it keeps them from moving on.

Another reason that people often start wishing for their exes to return is fear. They might have low self-esteem, or perhaps they've been in the dating scene for longer than they'd like without finding anyone interesting. They start becoming afraid that they'll never find anyone else, so they start to regret leaving their past relationship.

There's that nasty combo again: fear and regret.

When you feel the creeping of regret, remember that there is something to discover from every experience. You learn from every relationship how to act in the next one. You grow. If you've chosen someone who needs you to rescue or repair them, hopefully you then learn to seek out balanced and loving partners.

I believe that choosing partners that need to be rescued is a lack of self-love. You see a fixer-upper and subconsciously (or maybe even consciously) think, *Oh,* that *is the kind of person I deserve love from.* No, darling, no. You deserve to be adored, treasured, and inspired! You've just temporarily forgotten that, while here on planet Earth.

If you've been praying for your ex to come back into your life, I'd like to make a very loving suggestion to you. Put a pause on that particular request from Heaven, and try using the following prayer instead . . .

Dear God,

I'm feeling a pull to return to my ex. I'd like to have clarity on why that is. Help me to remember all the reasons I left. Help me to have a clear understanding as to why I might have this desire. If returning to my ex is only based on fear, then alleviate that fear, cut my energetic connection to my ex, and show me clearly the joy that's possible for me in a relationship with someone else.

Then, stand back and see, feel, hear, and understand the truth of your desire. Use your magical Genie powers to divine the answers you need to get back out of the lamp, because that's what's happened here. Your fear and regret have put you back into the lamp, and *that* is why you're not manifesting your next, and vastly improved, partner!

Let your past (and your ex) go.

BRING IN THE LOVE . . . IT'S AS EASY AS 1, 2, 3!

— The **first** step to bringing romance into your life is to get clear on what you're looking for. It's important to have clarity on what parts of past romances you would like to have back and what parts you want nothing to do with. (At the end of this chapter, I've included some exercises to help you get that clarity.)

— **Second**, get *out* there! You know where—out in the world! I'm eternally stunned by the number of people who ask me when they will meet their soul mate. I'll ask, "What are you doing to reach out to them?"

The answer will nearly always be, "Nothing."

So I ask, "Well, are you out there, meeting people?" The answer is almost invariably, "No"!

This is a strategy that works just dandy if your soul mate is the FedEx delivery person and you order a *lot* of stuff. Otherwise, it's not such a great plan.

You have to shine your light! You have to be out where you can be found! It's also a great way to refocus your sights away from the past and the ex to the future and the endless opportunities that can be found on a planet with 7.5 billion people on it!

— **Third** . . . be in joy! Be in anticipation! Be confident and certain that all those feelings that I mentioned at the beginning of this chapter are meant to be yours. Positive emotions are the magnets to manifesting your heart's desire, especially when it comes to love.

Let me say that again.

Positive emotions are the magnets to manifesting your heart's desire, especially when it comes to love.

You have to find your personalized way of bringing forth those happy emotions of faith, whether it's singing love songs at the top of your lungs, reading joyful poetry, creating a very romantic vision board, or just asking your angels to let you feel the eager anticipation of what is sure to be yours.

Try to embrace this notion. If you have an open heart and you're full of love to give . . .

YOU. WILL. FIND. LOVE.

Heaven won't let all your love go to waste. Love is the most precious thing in the Universe.

I'm always telling clients that when romance comes into their lives, everything else goes on hold. That's why I never mind telling someone that their romantic partner isn't going to arrive for 4 or 8 or even 12 months. "Do other things," I tell them. "Get stuff done! Once the romance shows up, all you'll care about is looking into dreamy eyes. So take the time you have before they show up to get done whatever you need to do." I mean, seriously . . . when you're in the process of falling in love, all that matters is that next text, next e-mail, next phone call.

If you're wanting romance in your life right now, but the primary focus of your Genie magic is on career, it may take longer. Most people can handle only so much at once. If your career, a health issue, or some other thing is taking all your time, energy, and Genie magic, it shouldn't be surprising that romance isn't popping into your life. Finish what you're working on, and then take a break. Recharge your Genie batteries, and then focus on your romantic life. You'll be surprised just how quickly things happen when your focus turns to love!

WHEN THE MAGIC IS OUT OF BALANCE

When we first fall in love, it's very easy for relationships to be out of balance. We can be so goo-goo over someone that we stop taking care of ourselves. At first, maybe that's not so horrible. But here's the rub: it can become a habit. Before you know it, you're giving 75 percent, to your beloved's 25 percent of giving back. Then your partner slowly starts to *expect* you to do that.

When the magic between two Genies is out of balance, unhappiness is the eventual result. If you try to correct the balance, the other person can resent it. Remember what I said before: people often don't like it when you change, especially if that change involves you doing less for them.

It's crucial to stay balanced from the beginning of a relationship. A good way to do that is to talk honestly and openly with a trusted friend about how the giving and receiving in the relationship is going. You need someone objective and kind who can listen and then gently point out to you if things are a little out of balance.

Also, consider the possibility that you're the type who attracts drama masters. Remember them from the previous chapter? These are the people who will let you work your magic for them till it hurts and even then expect more. Again, that's why it's so critical early on in a relationship to make sure things are balanced. If you're behaving in a balanced way, then even if you've just found yourself another drama master and you don't give, they'll probably go away.

A strong social network will help you release a drama master. When you have the support of your friends, it's easier to remember that you don't need that relationship. After all, you've most likely done it over and over. Why would you want someone who doesn't value you enough to love you in a balanced and fair way? Is romance *really* worth so much to you that you'll take it from just anyone?

Now here's the crazy part. You may be thinking about what I just asked you and realizing that you seriously don't know the answer to that question. But I bet you dollars to doughnuts that you're also the very same person who would tell your friends that they're crazy for dating that drama master. Right?

Let's say you're already down that rabbit hole. You're hitched up to a drama master, and you've been giving too much for too long. You know it. Your friends know it. In fact, everyone on the planet knows it *except* your partner. Now what do you do?

Well, my dear, sweet friend, it's time to *renegotiate* your Genie love contract.

To start, make a list of all the things that you do to further the relationship. Then make another list of what your partner does. Now it's time to have a conversation to move some of the things from *your* list to your partner's. Consider it balancing the scales.

I know from experience that this will be a delicate discussion. People don't like it when you change, especially if that change means fewer things being done on their behalf. So I highly recommend using soft voices, taking small steps, and, of course, acknowledging the things your partner actually does.

If you can't think of *anything* your partner does to support you and your relationship, then maybe you have more to think about than just how unbalanced your relationship is—like whether you're even in a relationship at all or if you've just fallen into the category of unpaid Genie servant. If that's the case, think about what you would tell a friend in that situation. And then look at yourself in the mirror and repeat.

THE THING ABOUT LIFE PARTNERS

I have a very close friend that I've known for decades. I want to protect her privacy, so let's just call her "Cyndi." Cyndi and I freely share what is going on in our personal and professional lives with each other. As many do, Cyndi laments that her relationship with her husband, "Paul," doesn't feel very much like a soul-mate relationship. From an emotional standpoint, things seem uneven to her. In fact, it's pretty uneven all the way around. That doesn't make Paul a bad guy. Cyndi loves him very much, and they're committed to one another. It's just that Paul is emotionally capable of giving only so much, and Cyndi is capable of far, far more.

So Cyndi loves Paul, and Paul loves Cyndi. He is getting most, if not all, of his needs met, but she is not. She has also come to the conclusion that it is unlikely that she is ever going to get what is missing from her life from Paul.

Over the years, this has naturally led to many, many long phone calls between Cyndi and me to discuss whether she should strike out on her own again in hopes of finding that heart-to-heart soul-mate connection she very much desires but doesn't have, nor can realistically expect to have, with Paul.

There has never been a clear answer to this question, by the way. That being said, an interesting epiphany presented itself while processing this dilemma recently.

As a life partner, Paul is pretty cool. He and Cyndi laugh a lot. They love their kids and are awesome parents. They have a beautiful home and travel all the time. They get along very well and have moments that are clearly special. They have been there for one another through some pretty dark times. And there is *love*.

Paul doesn't feel to Cyndi like a soul mate. But he *does* feel like a very valuable life partner. And is that so bad? (Of course, in this case, only Cyndi can answer that. And it's possible that she is getting close to answering it just by seeing Paul in the category he more honestly belongs in—and that he can *excel* in.)

By seeing our romantic partners as they *are* instead of spending a lot of time comparing them to what we might *want* them to be, we can get a lot of clarity. By looking at the dynamics between the people in the relationship and noting what is present rather than what is absent, there's the possibility for peace.

Of course, some needs are "must-haves," and that's a very personal, individual assessment. If those are missing, then even the most amazing of life partners won't be enough.

Nevertheless, I submit this concept of soul mates and life partners to you in hopes that a new perception of things might bring clarity and peace into a situation in your own life, whether past or present.

One other thing, though, before we move on: In my original definition of *soul mates*, I said that they are often here to help us learn something and evolve. And sometimes that can make us crazy.

Under that definition, it's possible, just possible, that Paul is a soul mate, after all.

WOUNDS THAT LINGER

It is said that "time heals all wounds," and that's true more often than not. But it's fair to say that some wounds are deeper than others. Some *linger*. You may think the loss or pain has healed and forgiveness has done its thing, and then, out of nowhere, you suddenly realize that the wound is still there.

That's *so* annoying.

There are losses I've experienced in my life that linger, but they don't keep me from living a magical life. Of all the gifts I've been given, the one I cherish the most is that of faith. My spiritual belief system, wherever it came from, is strong. I believe in a loving Universe. I believe in angels. I believe that I'm watched over by those I have lost, and even those whose names are lost to me in this incarnation. I truly believe that everything in my life has happened for a reason, whether I know what that reason is or not. I believe that this life is an illusion and happens in the blink of an eye; when it's over, we go back "home" to Heaven and say to ourselves, "Wow! What an amazing ride!" Then we get right back in line to come here again.

Even though that last little bit sounds crazy to me, I still believe it's true. I believe this existence is precious beyond words to our souls, even if we don't know it while we're here. This gift of faith allows me to mourn my losses, to go through whatever tragically beautiful event has presented itself, and to stay my course. To keep going. To keep believing.

Some of the deepest, longest-lingering wounds can come from romantic love. Very often—though not always—a new love brings recovery from love lost. But the arrival of a new relationship can be held up if a wound from your past hasn't healed. So let's talk about why that happens.

ORIGINS OF THE WOUNDS

Fear. Obsession. Unforgiveness. These are the barriers to recovery. This is why the wounds linger. The Genie magic machine is taking its instructions from those three negative emotions and accompanying thoughts. They become the irritants that keep your wounds open, your heart closed, and your opportunities to love again out of reach.

— First of all, the root of all unhealed wounds is **fear**. You may fear that the love you've lost is the best or only love you'll ever experience. If you ended the relationship, then you may be afraid that you made a mistake in doing so. You might become certain that as time goes by, you'll truly never love again. Your fear causes you to believe that the one that got away was your first and best opportunity for happiness, and now you've ruined it.

These kinds of beliefs run your heart around in circles. And if you believe them, then your ability to heal is halted because your Genie magic is busy, busy, busy making those beliefs the truth. The more you hurt, the more you push away new opportunities for love. That might be a conscious choice, if you've decided never to fall in love again so that you can be safe from being hurt again. More often, however, it's a subconscious choice. The circular thinking keeps you focused on your wound, you metaphorically pick at it, and it never heals. It never stops hurting. It's always there, you're always aware of it, and your Genie magic does its thing. Energetically, you're not available to other people, and those who might be drawn to you are instead pushed away.

— As you think of the past and relive it, this can become **obsession**. As time goes by, even that person who was making you miserable might transform in your mind into the lover of your dreams who brought you moments of happiness you'll never see again.

— And finally, there can be **unforgiveness**. All you see is what your past lover did wrong or what you yourself did wrong. You may or may not forgive them. (If you choose not to, this can lead to anger that rests in your heart unresolved.) But more often, what I see are people who have never forgiven themselves, especially if they were the ones who ended the relationship. Even if they didn't, their egos are more than happy to remind them of all the things they did wrong that pushed their beloved away. But it doesn't have to be that way.

Healing the Wounds

Remember the corkscrew of emotions that we talked about back in Chapter 1? When your thoughts are negative, your emotions follow. Well, it's time to unwind all these emotions. Because fear is the root of all of these, let's unwind them in reverse order.

— **Forgiveness** must happen—we've already talked about that. However, in this instance, consider framing it this way: If the person you're insisting on not forgiving desperately wants your forgiveness, then perhaps they deserve to have it. If they couldn't care less whether you forgive them, then holding on to your anger isn't hurting them at all anyway.

Now, let's just say your ex was a real jerk—gave you really good reasons to be mad. Which person do you think they most likely are: the one wanting your forgiveness or the one who couldn't care less? Either way, who's being hurt the most by the lack of forgiveness? If you're thinking it's anyone other than you, then trust me . . . you're fooling yourself.

Even more important is *self*-forgiveness. Hear me, and hear me now. I don't know what happened in your past. I don't know the circumstances. But this I humbly believe: at any point in your life, you were doing the best you could. There's a reason for why your relationship ended, and it wasn't because you did something unforgivable. From Heaven's viewpoint, you are always forgivable. You're following a path. And even if you don't know it now, you're perfect and beautiful and deserving of the greatest of love and the most powerful grace and forgiveness that God or Spirit or the Universe—whatever name you prefer—has to bestow upon you. And so who are *you* not to forgive someone as beautiful and amazing as you? Let it go. Release it. Forgive yourself.

— Now on to the **obsession**. I find that obsession with the past and/or the past lover tends to fade with the acceptance of forgiveness and the diminishing of fear. So, in a way, think of it as a symptom of the wound. Still, obsessive thoughts can be really tricky to get under control. To help you out, there's a Genie Academy lesson at the end of this chapter that just might allow you to break that cycle.

— And, finally, let's talk about that **fear**. I'm going to give you something to think about here. A new way of perceiving the love that was lost. So, please, pay attention to this, because it's important. Remember how I told you before that if you experienced true and powerful love, then that ability is within *you*. I don't care who your partner was; your experience on this planet is the one that *you* and that Genie within you were creating. You created that experience of mighty and powerful love. You magically brought that passion into your life. You created the opportunity and the space that allowed that feeling of being loved to happen. And if *you* created it, what does that say?

It means you can create it *again*. It's within you to make a new Genie wish. You have all the magic you need to have true and mighty love in your life. Fear is pointless.

So again . . .

Love is infinite. Love is eternal.

And you? You're a magical Genie who's made of love.

* *

$\mathcal{G}$ENIE $\mathcal{A}$CADEMY

Lesson #16: Write Your Own Romance

When I was single, I happened across a picture of someone in a magazine that made my heart do a little jump. For whatever reason, the image got stuck in my mind, and I would find myself daydreaming about what I'd do if I were to meet this person. That's when I started writing my own romance stories not only as a way to get clear as to what I was looking for romantically but also as a way of manifesting it.

Get yourself a notebook or journal that is dedicated to your romance stories. It isn't necessary to have a picture, but if you do happen to have one of someone who strikes your fancy, glue the picture on the first page of the story you're going to write. Where do you imagine meeting this person? What would they be like? How would your first interaction go? Let your imagination run wild as you write the story of your first encounter.

Sometimes the tale for me would be written like a short story. Other times, it would come out like a diary entry. So long as the story is a joyful one and makes you feel happy and hopeful, you can consider your romance story a bestseller!

✦ ✦ ✦

Lesson #17: Let It Go

Sometimes it can be really difficult to release an ex or just someone you've become a little obsessed with. Here is a way to help release that person from your mind so that you can move on.

Take something that reminds you of the person you're having trouble releasing and put it in a little box. The item doesn't have to be anything big or fancy, nor do you need a fancy box. Just tie up the box with a little string, then bury it.

I suggest burying the box somewhere out of sight, like perhaps in a park or forest that you don't visit often. What you're doing here is burying the obsession. Then, in your mind, imagine the person you're stuck on walking away from you. Every time you think of that person again, imagine them farther and farther away.

When I once did this for myself, I eventually imagined my ex walking all the way to the Pacific Ocean, and then boarding a boat and sailing away!

CHAPTER 10

WHEN THE MAGIC DOESN'T SEEM TO WORK

Things don't always turn out the way we hope. That's just life. As the famous line adapted from the Robert Burns poem points out, "The best-laid plans of mice and men often go awry." It's just a fact that sometimes life zigs left when we had every intention for it to zag right.

When that happens, perhaps the most common thing people ask is, "Why?" Frankly, I think that's an excellent question! But you have to be careful not to go into a victim mentality when asking. It's pretty easy to begin to feel bad for yourself when life tosses those proverbial lemons your way, especially if you were very much looking forward to oranges.

I ask why *a lot*. But I always try to do so from the objective standpoint of curiosity. I keep saying that I genuinely believe that the Universe loves you beyond words. (And I'm going to *keep* saying it until it sinks in for you!) All the Divine wants is to make you happy. If you ask for oranges and get lemons, then there must be a reason why oranges would not have optimized your chances at happiness. If you believe that, if you hold on to that kind of faith, then it becomes a whole lot easier to navigate through a change of course.

THE MEANING BEHIND DETOURS
AND COURSE CORRECTIONS

When things don't go the way I had anticipated, I immediately start scanning for the new path that Heaven feels is better for me. Sometimes, a detour is itself a sign from Heaven, especially if there's only one alternative path available. But if multiple paths are present, or if my original plan can still be salvaged, I start asking Heaven and the angels for clear and concise directions. I tell them: "Show me the way to go, and I'll go there."

On countless occasions, my own personal plans didn't go the way I had intended. Some of these situations were very small, and others felt pretty significant at the time. In the end, almost all the outcomes turned out better than I had dreamed. Sometimes I can immediately come up with a reason why something had to happen. Other times, the epiphany can take a while.

I don't mean to oversimplify things here, but let's just say that, in general, we have two options: We can view a situation that didn't go as we had hoped negatively, or we can view it with an optimistic perspective like, "Wow, God must really have something fabulous in mind for me if there's something better than what I was dreaming of! Okay, I'm ready! Show me this new-and-improved plan!"

Sometimes Heaven is waiting for you to make changes within yourself that are necessary for you to be in energetic alignment with your desires. If your plans aren't going the way you want, then ask yourself: Is there something that you know in your heart you should be changing but aren't? Are there new, bold versions of yourself just waiting for you to embrace them, yet you're resistant?

If so, I once again ask you to ask the question: *Why?*

Heaven loves you. Your angels love you. God loves you. If you believe that, then there simply isn't any other logical explanation for a detour on your path other than that a more joyful destination than the one you had planned is waiting for you.

So, yes, when things don't go right, ask why. But do it with bright-eyed optimism, knowing that something much better is intended for you.

Trust in the love of Heaven to guide you along the path of joy.

WHEN SIGNS POINT TO "NO"

As you know, I put a great deal of faith in synchronicities and what I perceive to be messages from the angels. And so it's natural that when things aren't working out for us, one of the things we start to believe is that our plans are flawed. That Spirit must be telling us to change course. We must be on the wrong path. But that's not always the case!

When things get difficult, it's *possible* that you're getting signs from Heaven that you're headed in the wrong direction. Sometimes, however, life's challenges might be meant to embolden you, make you stronger, and solidify your resolve. It could be the beginning of something wonderful!

The trouble can be knowing how to tell whether your angels are giving you guidance on how to proceed versus a gentle message informing you that an entire new plan would serve you better.

Well, the answer is this simple: *it's in your heart.* And I truly mean that.

Your heart will never mislead you when it comes to your life purpose. Your heart will let you know when a dream is off path rather than just needing a little adjustment. Your heart will tell you when something is meant to be and when something better is waiting for you just out of sight. Even if there's sadness for what is not to be, there will be hope for what *will* be.

Your ego, on the other hand, will lie, lie, lie. It will tell you that you're not good enough. It will leave you feeling like a failure and tell you that you were foolish for even trying. These hurtful and mean messages aren't of the heart. Nor are they messages from your angels. Your angels will never, ever speak to you in that way. That's how you can tell when a message is from your ego versus Divine Guidance.

If something is not meant to be, something else will be offered. It may not happen in that moment, but it *will* happen soon. Before long you'll know that you were right to stop.

If you're supposed to keep going, when you look into your heart, it will sing you a song of determination! Ask your angels, and they will give you signs to keep going even through adversity.

People often ask me what it means when they seem to be getting messages that say both "yes" and "no" at the same time. In my experience, if you're getting "yes" more than "no," then you move forward! You treat the "no" messages as minor course corrections or lessons you needed in order to be successful in the future. It's when there aren't "yes" messages, only "no" messages, that you should consider a new path.

And if you *are* going to consider a new path, then do it with faith! Do it with hope! Do it with the knowing that the Universe loves you, and if your current plans aren't working—and your heart and angels confirm that you are to stop—then there's truly, absolutely, without a doubt something better waiting for you! This is simply the way the Universe works, so you must believe! Ask Archangel Jophiel to keep your thoughts positive and your hopes high; then stand back and watch as the magic happens.

If you're certain in your heart that you are to move forward, my advice is still the same: Do it with faith, hope, and the knowledge that the Universe loves you and the reason for these bumps in the road will make themselves clear as you continue along your journey.

You're a Divine child of God. A magical spark from the fire of the Universe. Whatever is happening in your life is meant to eventually lead you toward joy. Embrace your birthright.

DON'T GIVE UP!

So let's pretend that you've been trying and trying, but things just aren't working out for you. No matter what you do, you feel as though you're banging your head against a wall. Every direction you take shows you a new obstacle. It just seems like your plans are doomed. So what do you do?

It's okay if, sometimes, you get tired; that's only human. Experiencing a momentary lack of faith is only human. Losing the will to continue to pursue your dreams . . . even that can also be very human.

All this raises an interesting question: Are we *really* human?

It's been said that we're not human beings having a spiritual experience, but spiritual beings having a human experience. I fully believe that to be true. And so can it really be said that it's in our truest of true natures to not persevere? Aren't we here to shine our lights in such a way that the miracles we seek are always possible?

Aren't we ourselves miracles? And, therefore, miracle workers?

I believe that in our most challenging moments, we're meant to forge on. This is when we should redouble our efforts and fortify our determination to make a difference in our own lives as well as those around us. This is when we absolutely cannot give up!

Not too long ago, I was having a bad morning. Nothing too serious, just one of those days. As I began my daily prayers and meditations, I had this moment where I didn't feel like it was the right time to be praying. I just wasn't in the right energetic space for it. What I heard in my head next was: *Then this is exactly the time you* should *be praying.*

Now that first inclination not to pray? That was ego. That was the voice of isolationism in the face of challenge. The second voice? That was my guardian angel. (It could have also been my higher self, but I'm pretty good at picking out Joshua's voice after all these years.)

When we really don't feel like praying is, perhaps, exactly when we *should* be praying with the most diligence. The same goes for when we're experiencing challenges in life and just want to quit. It is in the moment when we would like to surrender that we must forge on. Of course, it can be hard to find the energy to do so at that moment. So what to do then?

Here's a little Genie analogy: When a car gets stuck, one of the things that people do is get assistance. They find someone to help them rock the car back and forth until they get enough momentum going to push it past whatever is holding it in place. Well, in the same way, you can ask your Genie group to help you. You can even magically do it for yourself by tackling whatever has you stuck step by step. The point is to do whatever it takes to get past the hump.

Don't forget the power of gratitude. Expressing what you're grateful for in your life can truly help you to spiral upward instead of downward. It can help you pick yourself up and get going again.

If your dream is stalled, then what I have to say to you is this: *Do. Not. Quit.*

You can't quit. You can't stop. You have to keep going. If you're passionate about a cause or dream, then you're meant to follow it wherever it takes you. You cannot stop pursuing your passion. You cannot stop reaching every single day for your calling. To do so is to quite literally be less than who you truly are.

Our dreams are what define us. They're what make us little tiny, magical bits of God. They're what make us miracle workers.

Never stop going after your dreams. You've got to make the miracle happen. Don't give up!

WHEN WISHES COLLIDE

Genies are more known for making wishes come true for other people than for themselves. No doubt, there will be people in your life for whom you would like to help make a wish come true. And you can do that! (Sometimes.)

Everyone has free will. That's the way Source made us, and that's the way we are. So no matter how well-intentioned you are—and even if the wish you have for someone else really *is* in their best interest—if the other person is not on board with the wish, it is unlikely you're going to get anywhere. Your magic will hit their resistance and fall flat on the floor.

I know from firsthand experience how distressing that is. It is especially distressing if the person you'd like to help very much *wants* your help! Let me share an example with you . . .

Jack and Jill are married. Jill is an excellent Genie! She is in touch with her Divine magic and has become really good at creating her own magical life. Jack, on the other hand . . . well, not so much.

Jack has been out of work for over a year now. At first he tried hard to find employment, but nothing ever seemed to pan out.

Over time, he became discouraged. His thoughts became very negative, and he felt close to succumbing to depression.

Jill desperately wants to help her husband, and Jack desperately wants her help! While he doesn't really understand all this "Genie stuff," he can't help but admit that she seems to be able to magically create whatever she wants. Naturally, Jack is completely on board with whatever Jill can do to help him manifest a job.

So what's the problem, you ask? Jill wants to help. Jack wants her to help. That should be enough! Right?

Wrong.

Remember, Genie wishes react to thoughts and emotions. Consciously, Jack may want Jill's help, but his thoughts on the topic of employment are totally negative. His emotions are ones of hopelessness and despair. Poor Jack has no idea that his inner magic is actually working at full power to respond to his inner condition, ensuring that no job comes. Every hour of every day he is focused on the lack of a job. That's the equivalent of Jack wishing for no job while Jill wishes for him to have one.

This is what happens when wishes collide. As I said, it can be heartbreaking.

Most of the time, this kind of compulsive negativity starts in the mind and then spreads to the emotions. To get out of it, it often works best to start working with your emotions because emotions are a reflection of your thoughts. You'll unwind the corkscrew, as I described in Chapter 1.

Jack's thoughts are pretty committed to the belief that there are no jobs out there. But his emotions can be brought out of the depressive feelings by getting him to think about something—*anything*—else that makes him happy. It will probably take time, constant effort, and, above all, Jack's cooperation. If Jill can get him to grasp the basics of being his own Genie, then together they can begin by focusing on just trying to keep the happy feelings coming. Baseball games, antique-car shows, time spent with friends (preferably hilarious friends) . . . just keep the happy moments coming.

When Jack's emotional condition starts to spiral upward, *then* Jill can start to work on his thoughts. *But not too fast!* One baseball game probably isn't going to create an emotionally stable Jack. He'll be happy during the game, but the moment his thoughts turn back to employment, he'll crash like a lead balloon.

The plan is to get Jack emotionally optimistic enough that he can grasp the concept that life isn't all that bad. That there's more to life than your job. Something is bound to come around at the right time because, "Hey. The Universe loves me." If Jack can get to that point, then Genie Jill will have a job lined up for him in no time!

Then the wishes won't be colliding—they'll be coinciding!

RE-MOTIVATE!

As you know, your inner Genie is pretty amazing! However, the magic you're weaving almost always requires action. So if you're having trouble getting the action part working, the magic part is definitely going to be slow.

Motivation can be elusive. You're all ready to write that great American inspirational novel, but instead you find yourself ticking off minor items from your to-do list, checking in on your friends on social media, or just plain staring at your computer screen trying to come up with that perfect next word. You tell yourself that just as soon as you have all the laundry folded, you'll tackle that chapter you've been procrastinating finishing.

But you have a lot of laundry. And days go by fast. Before you know it, another week has passed without so much as a new paragraph having been added to your manuscript.

Now, I'm a writer. So I've used this example purely as a metaphor for any project, creative endeavor, or passion that you want to get moving on but just can't seem to make any progress on. And, yes . . . the person in the scenario I just described is sometimes me. I have days when I can't type fast enough! And then I have days when I have this deep, burning desire to reorganize my closet.

So let me give you a couple of my tips on how to finally get moving when everything just feels stuck:

— First of all, ask for help of the human or the angelic kind. Being held accountable to someone is a great motivator, so call a friend or peer and tell them that you absolutely have to finish a certain amount of work today and that you've been procrastinating. Also, asking for angelic help can be amazing! Archangel Gabriel is one of my go-tos because she is great at helping you to get things done. I ask her for assistance when I just can't seem to get going.

— Another thing I do is to go after the project or to-do list item that I'm dreading the most and do it first. Get it out of the way! You can promise yourself all kinds of lovely goodies and rewards if you just finish those 300 words that you set as a goal or make those phone calls about renting space in a healing center. Whatever it is you've been putting off because you don't feel "in the mood"—get it done. Then everything gets a whole lot easier!

GENIE ACADEMY

Lesson #18: Gratitude Is the Fuel of the Universe

Gratitude is a very powerful part of your Genie magic. It is a manifesting tool and an essential part of prayer. Being thankful for what you already have just spins your energy in a positive, upward direction that, in turn, brings more positive things into your life.

Take a moment now to say thank you not just to friends, family, and people in your life, but also to God, the angels, and any loved ones in Heaven you believe watch over you. You can do this in writing, out loud, or in your head. Try to take some time every day to offer thanks to someone new. (You can set yourself a note to do so, like the Daily Magic Reminders in Lesson #10.)

Don't forget the importance of having gratitude for yourself. Make a list in your head of the reasons why you're grateful for *you!* Even if you have to "hitch" it to someone else, it's a start.

For example, say to yourself, "I'm grateful for me because otherwise my kids would not have someone wonderful to teach them right from wrong." Eventually, I want you to be able to say (and believe), "I'm grateful for me because I am *amazing*!"

Gratitude is the fuel of the Universe . . . keep your tank full and you'll go very far!

* *

CHAPTER 11

GENIE JOY

You may have noticed that I've spent a lot of time in this book encouraging you to take actions that will make you happy. The reason for that is simple: joy is a key method to gaining access to—and fully utilizing—your Genie magic. If being happy isn't the centerpiece to living a magical life, then what's the point?

So, now I'm going to tell you something that you might find challenging. Happiness . . . is a choice. Now I know, I know . . . you may have just groaned, grimaced, or rolled your eyes. But really, hear me out.

Our emotional well-being is largely a matter of perception. If we perceive that the things around us are unpleasant or "bad," then our emotions will respond in kind. We will feel sadness, anxiousness, and even anger. This in turn furthers our perceptions that the world is against us, and we become even *more* unhappy. It's a circle.

Likewise, happiness is circular. If we perceive that the Universe really does loves us, if we see the challenging things that happen in our lives as just temporary road markers meant to guide us in a better direction, then it becomes possible to recognize how treasured we are by the Divine. We may need to take a deep breath and whisper a prayer to Heaven for strength, but we don't have to allow our view of our lives to spiral downward.

To do this takes focus, determination, and, above all, vigilance in remaining aware of the illusion of entrapment that your ego just loves to serve up to you on a spoon. This life is a dreamlike experience full of distractions and endless to-do lists that can keep you from being aware of any particular moment. And yet, the power lies within each moment that you're choosing to be happy.

THE SIGNAL OF THE ROTTEN TOMATO

I want to share an analogy with you. It's a very silly analogy, but I really like how it makes the point.

Let's pretend that you're in a maze. Imagine one of those big hedge mazes you might see in movies or on college campuses. Let's also say you're not quite sure where you are, but you do know it's not where you want to be.

As you move through the maze, God decides to drop a big, smelly, rotten tomato down from Heaven right in your path. Well! That's a fine how-do-you-do, right? *Doesn't God know that I'm headed somewhere? Don't my angels know I don't have time for this? Am I expected to clean up this mess?! This is utterly unfair—why does nothing in my life ever go the way I want it to?*

But you *are* in a maze. A big one! A gigantic maze called life. You're always trying to find your way to the center where the prize is, or maybe you're just seeking a way out.

So what if I told you that the whole purpose of that tomato from Heaven is to help you. What if the rotten tomato is just God sending you the following message:

> *"Hey. You're walking in the wrong direction. Where you're headed won't make you happy. Turn around and go back the other way. I'll send more tomatoes as necessary to guide you. Or, if you'll keep your perceptions positive and trust me, I'll drop some white angel feathers for you to follow, instead. Your choice. Either way, I love you. And I'm going to get you out of this maze one way or another. No matter how stubborn you are about this, I'm going to find a way to lead you toward joy."*

Now think about this: the Source of everything we know loves you so much that it took the time to throw a rotten tomato your way, just to get you to turn around and head in a happier direction.

How utterly beloved are you? How treasured. How adored!

I'm not saying you have to love rotten tomatoes, nor am I saying you have to love it when things happen that just don't feel great. But what I *am* saying is that in any given moment, you can hold up your arms to Heaven and say:

"Okay, okay. I didn't like that. But I trust you. I know you love me. I get it. I'm not trapped here. No person or thing can keep me from finding a way to make my dreams come true. So bring on the tomatoes, though if it's all the same to you, I'm officially now placing my order for white feathers, instead. Show me what direction to go."

If you can just grasp this concept of ultimate love no matter what is happening in your life—if you can embrace this practice of faith—then you'll have far greater power over your own happiness than you can possibly imagine.

IF YOU'RE HAPPY AND YOU KNOW IT . . .

It has come to my attention over time that people don't always know it when they're happy.

I'm not talking about the "Oh, it's my birthday and I got nice presents today!" kind of happy. I think most of us have that kind of happy fairly well pinned down.

I'm talking about the big picture, standing back, broad brush, high-level-overview kind of happy. I'm talking about that "hindsight is 20/20" kind of happy. It's not a moment-by-moment gleeful pop-song type of joy, but more of a peaceful multiverse ballad. It's playing quietly in the background, so you may have gotten so used to it that you have forgotten how lovely the melody is.

Over the years, I've had many interactions with clients, friends, and even ghosts from the past who were spending time in the little land of regret. You already know I believe regret to be a wasted emotion that keeps you unable to move forward. Still, I'm by no means immune to it. Regret does occasionally exert its chilly grip over my thoughts, and when it does, I think, *Rotten tomatoes*. Then I push regret out of my mind.

However, in trying over time to reconcile myself to moments of regret in a way that would serve a purpose, I've found that the histories that they often represent are times in my life that I was pretty darned happy. I just wasn't fully aware of it.

We're always looking for the next big experience: "The grass is always greener" . . . yada yada, right? If we grow immune to the level of happiness we're living in, then naturally we start dreaming about how to get to the next level. This can cause us to not only become disgruntled with our current situation, but also bar us from seeing that things are actually pretty darned good right now.

Staying in a state of Genie joy requires regular gratitude assessments. Practice Lesson #18 regularly. Ask yourself: What are you happy for in your life right now? How is your life better today than it was in the past?

I still encourage you to continue to grow and reach for even more joy in your life at all times. However, it's also critical to be aware of the happiness you have in any given moment as a way to increase your chances at more happiness in the future.

After all, if you're focused on your happiness, more will come to you. That's just the way Genie magic works.

JOY REPELLENT

Have you come across people who just can't seem to be happy, no matter what? I'm sure you have. Perhaps there are even some in your life. They're often either alarmists or what I call "horriblizers." No matter what good thing might come into their lives, they manage to allow their minds to run away with horrible scenarios of all the things that might (and probably *will*) go wrong!

Not too long ago, my dear friend Samantha fell in love. It was magical but also quite unexpected. Frankly, she had given up on finding love and happiness in the city we lived in, so she was on her way out of town.

You know what happened next, right?

Wham! She met someone and fell immediately head over heels in love. I was rather happy about this because I hoped that meant my friend might not leave town after all! However, the more curious reactions came from the naysayers: "Don't change your plans," they said. "This is probably just a fling. You should just go ahead and move." Others told her, "You're too much of a romantic. You expect too much." And, of course, there was the quiet snarkiness of rolled eyes.

While chatting with Samantha about all of this, she said to me: "Why can't these people be happy? It's like they're walking around with joy repellent on them!"

In that moment, I thought, *Oh my God, that's it! Joy repellent!* Can't you just imagine a giant spray can with a big yellow frowny face on the front? The label would say Joy-B-Gone! Ads would proclaim it: "The perfect protection against being disappointed, getting your heart broken, or other possible causes of tears."

Joy repellent is a way of subduing risks. It may make you feel safe, but it also robs you of your reasons for being in this life. We've *all* been hurt at one point or another. Samantha has been hurt many times. (Sometimes I've been there and seen it happen.) But, as Samantha pointed out in our conversation, she'd rather feel the joy and excitement of love for just a few minutes and then suffer a possible heartbreak than to never have felt it at all. She was willing to take a leap of faith.

The path to Genie joy is to go after what you want with wild abandon even if you're afraid—even if there's risk. Even if the joy could be temporary. You have no way of knowing if the joy will last unless you give it a go!

This world is a playground. Granted, there are times when it's a pretty freaky playground, but we're here to create. We're here to open our arms to experiencing joy, not to inoculate ourselves from it for fear that we might find ourselves hurting later. A magical life comes from having a vision of a happier *you* and being willing to risk going after it.

So here's my question for you: Do you have on Joy-B-Gone? Are you avoiding living for fear of hurting? Because, let me tell you this little secret about joy repellent . . . it washes off. You can make a different choice. You can take a leap of faith and chase after your joy.

MIRROR, MIRROR

An argument could be made that nearly everything we encounter in life is a mirror. If we're always creating our reality, then what else could our reality be but a reflection of our inner life?

Challenges from others can be exasperating, and sometimes the issues are all theirs. But more often than not, I find that whatever is tripping us up is some kind of mirror for the ways in which we're getting in our own way. Gaining clarity on that often makes the bothersome detail we'd been focused on just sort of fade away.

I don't always realize it at the time, but during moments of challenge or apprehension, I tend to stop breathing or breathe less deeply. Maybe you can relate to that. When we're worried or in fear, we tend to hold our breath.

But let's think about that for a second. If breath is life, and we arrest or lessen our breathing, then we stop living fully. We stop taking in all that life has to offer purely out of fear of what is next to come.

What we have to remember is that there's no plateau of happiness in life. There's only the place where we stop climbing the mountain. There's always a higher joy to reach for. There's always more that we can be.

To further that metaphor, the climb up the mountain enriches our life. The view becomes more and more spectacular. In many parables, there's a hermit at the top of the mountain. He is the pinnacle of spiritual knowledge and inner wisdom. If we continue to climb, we get to join him and shine our light for all to see. We become a beacon of encouragement to the world.

I have seen sorrow. I have seen heartbreak. But I've never seen any of it *not* lead to growth. I could tell you sad stories about my past, but what for? There's nothing in my life looking back that I would change, because I love my life now. Even in the midst of the saddest things that ever happened to me, I believe with all my heart that as long as I'm honest with myself . . . as long as I look truthfully into the "mirror, mirror" of my soul . . . as long as I keep climbing the mountain . . . I will always come to the same conclusion.

Everything that happens is meant to guide me to joy.

EMOTIONAL MEMORY

Memory is a powerful gift. We can use it to bring joy into an otherwise dreary day, or sadly, we can use it to be unkind to ourselves by dwelling on things that made us unhappy. There are two kinds of memory:

- *Intellectual memory*—this is the typical type that most of us immediately think of.

- *Emotional memory*—now, I'm not a psychologist, so this is just a term I use to refer to a way to bring happiness into our hearts when we're not really feeling joy at the moment.

Let me give you an example:

I adore Halloween! Seriously, it's one of those holidays that gets my inner child squealing with glee! And just so there's no misunderstanding, I do *not* like scary Halloween. Frankly, I don't like scary anything. The last time I watched a horror movie, I was a teenager. I learned right then and there that stuff like that just means three weeks of lost sleep and an even longer period of trying to get those images out of my head. I'll have none of that, thank you very much.

What I love is what a dear friend of mine termed "whimsical Halloween." I like five-year-old Halloween! During the season, my house is decorated with sparkly, happy jack-o'-lanterns that slowly turn all kinds of different colors. (Yes, glitter-covered jack-o'-lanterns . . . I'm sure you're shocked.)

I decorate my house so that children will run to it with glee, not approach it with uncertainty. I often dress as Peter Pan, the proverbial child who never grows up. I'm always prepared for hundreds of trick-or-treaters, because that's what I'm using all that Genie joy to manifest!

Hopefully that description gives you an idea about what I mean by emotional memory. I'm tapping into memories from the past—from my childhood, really—that make my heart just swell with happiness! That's the power of memory I'm referring to that can empower you to do amazing other things in our day-to-day lives.

One of the things that I caution against is romanticizing the past, but it isn't always a bad thing. Yes, sometimes seeing the past through rose-colored glasses can get in your way. That's particularly true if your image of the "good ol' days" is keeping you from moving forward.

But on the upside, there's something to be said for looking backward with a positive viewpoint that can heal the past. Sometimes seeing that there were forgotten special moments can really make a difference. If you can look backward and recognize that certain people in your life had better motives than you originally gave them credit for, you can become free of old wounds.

Looking backward and emotional memory are tied to one another. And when used incorrectly, they can do harm. If over time, your view of the past can become "horriblized," then wounds can deepen. If you're not careful, you can inflate past wrongdoings beyond what was reality. When you do this, you aren't hurting anyone but yourself. This turns into a challenge of forgiveness. And by now you know that unforgiveness grows like a cancer within you—not within anyone who may have done you wrong.

When happiness lives in your heart, your ability to use your Genie magic to manifest miraculous things is ramped all the way up! When your heart is filled with sadness, well . . . it can be hard to manifest a sandwich, let alone your fondest hopes and dreams.

So here's my recommendation . . . get into a regular practice of looking for joy in every part of your life. Remember happiness. Let your heart grow every day!

$\mathcal{G}$ENIE $\mathcal{A}$CADEMY

Lesson #19: Adding Up the Joy!

You'll need a pocket-size notebook—maybe the one you used back in Genie Academy Lesson #1. In that lesson, you were looking for the negative things you were unaware that you were saying to yourself. In this lesson, you're going to be looking for the positive things that happen all around you!

Start keeping track of every time something makes you smile. If some small event brings you joy—even for just a brief moment—make a note of it. If you overhear a joke being told that makes you laugh, write it down. Record everything that happens over a few days. For instance, when I see small children playing, it always makes me smile! Someone walking past me with a dog will always make my heart feel happy.

Now it's time to add up the joy! How many times were you happy each day while you kept a list? Did you notice that as you kept track, the number of times you were happy each day continued to rise? Did it almost become tiresome by the end of the experiment because you had so many things to write down?

If so, you are definitely doing it right!

AFTERWORD

The Genie-ous within You

We've almost come to the end of our magical Genie journey together. The things I have shared with you are the steps revealed to me over time that allowed me to leave a world where at first I was unhappy and alone. I once spent all my waking time trying to make other people happy, hid from who I truly was, and worked in a career that was hopelessly not "me." The concepts I have laid out for you allowed me to get in touch with my inner Genie so that I could completely transform my life into the magical one I live now, full of wonderful, loving people. I am my own, true, authentic self; I have the career of my dreams, which only keeps getting better and better; and I'm happy nearly all the time. Whatever dreams I still have, I am working on and watching them grow and bloom.

The beautiful part, which I hope you've gleaned by now, is that there is nothing in this magical guide that *you* can't also do. There is a magical Genie inside you as well, and it's nothing short of a Divine compass designed to lead you toward joy. In short, you're a magical Genie-ous, and you can make the magic happen in your life, too!

YOUR GENIE REVIEW

I have a few last thoughts for you, but first a little Genie review might be in order. So once again, here is a quick rundown of the things to keep in mind in order to have that magical life:

- Know that angels are real. They're there to help you, so let them. Discover your favorite way to start a dialogue with Heaven and keep talking!

- Start every morning by saying something wonderful to yourself. Affirm to yourself that today will be magical. Ask your angels to help guide you all day long in taking steps in the direction of happiness.

- Have **faith** that you are loved. (Remember, that word is in boldface because it should be thought of as a bold endeavor!) Believe that the Universe is constantly pushing you toward joy even if it doesn't feel like it. If you can fully grasp that, your life will immediately be better.

- Live each day as though every minute is magic, because it is. Follow your heart, but give your mind a say in things, as well.

- Stay awake! Look for the magic! Embrace the synchronicities! Look for the signs from Heaven, and talk back!

- Get control of your thoughts—and therefore your emotions—so that you can use your Genie magic to create what you desire instead of what you're afraid of.

- Don't judge yourself. Don't compare yourself to other people. Understand that every single day of your life you're doing the best you can. And the next day, you'll do better because you grew from yesterday. Be proud of you.

- Don't judge other people, either. Seriously. All that does is set you up for believing that others are probably judging you.

- Get regret, fear, and unforgiveness out of your life. They aren't serving you. Do whatever you need to do to heal those emotions and let them go.

- Remove drama from your life in all ways possible. If you're a drama-holic, then replace negative-based drama with happy drama. You'll get the same rush, but you'll be a whole lot happier!

- Release drama masters from your life. I know that you may have a spouse or a child for whom that's not possible. I get that. But be honest—there are people in your life right now who bring you all manner of annoyance whom you could release. Relationships that only take, take, take and never give back should be shown the door.

- Forgive, forgive, forgive. Others, yes, but most especially yourself. For everything.

- Be clear on what you're wishing for. Make *real* choices, not just what seems easiest at the time. Understand that you have your dreams for a reason, and you are meant to chase them!

- Follow your Divine guidance. Doing so will make you an energetic match for your dreams and give you direct access to your inner Genie and the magic to make your life amazing!

- Give yourself time to build up your faith in your ability to create the magical life you want. Start small if you have to, and build up your "faith muscles."

- Create groups of other Genies who can help you manifest your dreams. Help them in return.

- When the magic starts to take off, don't take on more than you can handle. Say yes to all your dreams—unless it's too much, then it's okay to say no or "not now."

- Do what makes you feel like a kid again, whatever that is. Ignore anyone who thinks you're being silly. In fact, I highly, *highly* recommend being silly.

- Laugh often. Laugh loud. At something. Anything. Most especially at yourself. Probably because of something you did while being silly.

- Make yourself your number one priority. As much as you can, every day.

- Love your family and let them love you. If you don't have that in your family of origin, then seek out a family of choice to support and cherish you.

- Always, always, always be your most true, authentic self. This is one of the most important, magical things you can do. I promise you it will improve your life in ways you can't imagine.

- No time traveling! If you live your life looking backward, then you're missing the now and you're not preparing for the future.

- Be grateful for at least one thing in your life at some point during the day. Gratitude is the fuel of the Universe. The more you fill up your tank with it, the farther you'll go.

- Make your space magical so that the energy in it helps propel you forward into the life you are dreaming of.

- Be kind to people. Practice random acts of magic. Smile at strangers. Most of them will smile back. Send angels of love to those who do not.

- Make friends with your body. Treat it well.

- Avoid, at all costs, doing something that you personally consider wrong. It doesn't matter what society thinks. It only matters that *you* think it's wrong. It just never goes well, and it tends to make you feel undeserving, which gets in the way of your magic.

- Surround yourself with people who are differently gifted from you. It will expand your horizons and create new opportunities for joy.

- Remember that your reality isn't the *only* reality. Keep your mind open to other people's viewpoints. You don't have to agree with them, but you don't necessarily have to fight with them, either. Channel your energy into peaceful activism instead if you feel guided.

- Don't, under any circumstances, give your power away to someone else. You're your own Genie, not someone else's.

- Allow for the possibility of romantic love in your life, but let go of the concept of "the perfect one." Instead, allow the Universe to bring you rich and joyful relationships that help you grow and become more and more who you truly are each day.

- Never give up! Go after every dream you have. Trust that if it doesn't work out, there is something better, and then go after *that* with all your passion.

- Love life. Love others. Love yourself.

THE STARS IN YOUR EYES

I freely admit that I have stars in my eyes. I see the world pragmatically, but in happy hues of hope. I'm aware of the challenges before the world—as well as me, personally—but I honestly believe that we're all loved by a Universe that adores us and wants us to find unlimited amounts of joy.

So why wouldn't I have stars in my eyes?

You know . . . you have stars in your eyes, too. I hope that you're aware of that. The people I meet sparkle right back at me when I'm teaching classes or in book-signing lines. They might even sparkle via the printed words on my social-media pages or by the sound of their voices when they call in to my radio show. The stars in your and my eyes sparkle with the magic that is within us, because magic always comes in sparkles.

I don't consider the stars in my eyes to be some sort of special gift. Those are standard issue for all of us. However, one of the gifts I do perceive that I have is the ability to see the beauty not just in life but also in every person I meet. I love this gift. It may well be my favorite gift that Heaven blessed me with. To be able to look at a person and see the magic within them and then, hopefully, to mirror it right back to them so that they can see how beautiful they are.

Do you know how beautiful you are?

Of course, it's possible you might have forgotten your sparkle power. If so, your stars are still there, but they're not shining because you're not focused on the magic of life that would make them shine. It is my most fervent prayer that in reading this book, you've at least started to remember about that power. If the stars in your eyes aren't shining right now, then I at least hope that there's a glimmer of Divine light starting to peek out.

If you haven't done your Genie Academy lessons, then I encourage you to go back now and do them. They are keys to transforming your life and your way of being in the world into the magic you were born to have. And as you transform, the light in your eyes will grow. What was just a glimmer before will become a field of bright, sparkling stars.

That's how we, those of us whose Genies are awake and making magic, will recognize each other—*by the stars in our eyes.*

There is nothing you can't have, nothing you can't do. You can have it all—and, I assure you, that's what God wants. God *wants* you to have it all. And that's how I know that . . .

Life is magic.

ACKNOWLEDGMENTS

Having a magical life is inseparable from the magical people who help make it possible. In my case, the blessings are endless. My deepest thanks to:

Doreen Virtue: Mentor, sister, and friend. I don't know what I did to deserve you . . . and as usual I find my gratitude has no words. So, I'll just say "pink snail in Italy" and leave it at that.

Reid Tracy, Patty Gift, and Alex Freemon: For continuing to believe in me and providing magical opportunities to experience the life of my dreams. I am so humbly grateful.

Louise Hay: For building the perfect safe haven for a Genie to do his magic. (I *really* should've given you my shoes.)

Nicolette Salamanca Young: I don't know if this book would ever have happened without you. Thank you for being my cheerleader, my coach, and now my friend.

Nancy Levin: You know what you did, and I will love you forever because of it.

Sherry Warren: For keeping my head above water, for talking me off ledges, for fiercely protecting me, and for "the vault."

John Holland, Denise Linn, and Neale Donald Walsch: Your writings changed my life and set me on the path toward magic. I will forever be grateful.

Michael David Virtue: Because you lovingly never let me get away with anything, and I seriously love that.

Lee Crump: For your love, and the ring, and for letting me be barefoot in Tiffany's. You make it possible for me to have this life.

Raven, Jace, and Riley: For unending magic, laughter, and joy.

Rhonda, Ted, Thaniel, and Keira Parolari, and Kristyn and Alex Bullard: For laughter. For always being there. For always making me feel safe and never alone. (Oh, and for Disney World.)

Wanda Valentine, Norma Lewis, and Luda Patton: Mother, aunt, and grandmama, respectively. I think they call it "unconditional love." Thank you for teaching me to believe.

Leah Lewis Paschel: You're my cousin and my "other sister." Thank you for loving me no matter how weird I got.

Dan Stone: Dear Sammie, thank you for being my soul mate and the "mirror me." Love, Serena.

Mark Isley, Jeff Gurney, and Mark Schaffer: For being the best brothers any guy could ever have. And for Spain. You are my very best wishes come true.

Luc Beaudoin, Raphael Cordova, and Ben Wankel: Because you just sort of got stuck with me, and you loved me anyway. You are all a precious part of my life.

Susan Dintino and Heather Hildebrand: For the prayers, the laughter, and making sure I don't forget who I am. You are my superhero sisters!

Eric Grauberger: Because I can literally say *anything*, and it's totally safe.

Robert Reeves: For being wise beyond your years and for making my sides hurt from laughing. Why is there never enough time?

Jason Garrett: For clarity on so many things, for silliness, and for never giving up on me.

Tanya Jahnke: For filling my home with magic and my heart with friendship. Love you, girl.

Nora and David Lasky: For making a *crazy* amount of dreams come true.

Michael Hobbs: For keeping me safe all those years and helping me to understand who I am.

Kim Goehring and Kay Sweeney: Because a sci-fi nerd needs friends.

Beth Urquhart: I couldn't have done any of this without you. I just couldn't have.

Greta Lipp, Mollie Langer, and Mairead Conlon: For being the very best event producers on the planet—and then my friends. Thank you for always, *always* making me feel special.

Mike Joseph, Rachel Fernandes, Mitch Wilson, Steve Morris, Rocky George, and everyone at Hay House Radio: For making *Magical Things* truly magical and so much fun for me. You rock!

Michelle Pilley, Jo Burgess, Julie Nolan, and the whole Hay House UK team: For always giving me a chance to sparkle.

Jennifer Simmons, Donna Abate, and Craig Johnson: For always treating a recovering certified public accountant (who didn't know what he was doing) like a total rock star. I will never forget.

Pat Blocker, Kathy Azcuenaga, and Dr. Julie Kelly: For making it possible for me to run all over the world knowing that my children are safe.

Patrina Odette: You are my dear friend, but you are also the most magical photographer. Thank you for always making me look my best.

Gregg Hoffman: Because having a magical life includes having a strong body and feeling good about yourself. You are the best personal trainer, *ever*!

ABOUT THE AUTHOR

Radleigh Valentine is a best-selling Hay House author of five tarot decks, one angel oracle deck, and two books. An internationally known spiritual teacher, he has spoken at more than 70 events in 10 countries since 2012, including over a dozen Hay House "I Can Do It" events. Radleigh is also a regular participant of the annual Hay House World Summit and is a frequent speaker at the Angel World Summit in London and Engelkongress in Germany and Austria.

His Hay House Radio show, *Magical Things with Radleigh Valentine*, is a mixture of teaching through laughter and poignant readings for listeners. His very popular video show, *Ask Rad!*, streams on Facebook and Instagram simultaneously each week.

Find out more about Radleigh at www.radleighvalentine.com and Facebook.com/RadleighValentine.

We hope you enjoyed this Hay House book. If you'd like to receive our online catalog featuring additional information on Hay House books and products, or if you'd like to find out more about the Hay Foundation, please contact:

Hay House, Inc., P.O. Box 5100, Carlsbad, CA 92018-5100
(760) 431-7695 or (800) 654-5126
(760) 431-6948 (fax) or (800) 650-5115 (fax)
www.hayhouse.com® • www.hayfoundation.org

✦ ✦ ✦

Published and distributed in Australia by:
Hay House Australia Pty. Ltd., 18/36 Ralph St., Alexandria NSW 2015
Phone: 612-9669-4299 • *Fax:* 612-9669-4144 • www.hayhouse.com.au

Published and distributed in the United Kingdom by:
Hay House UK, Ltd., Astley House, 33 Notting Hill Gate, London W11 3JQ
Phone: 44-20-3675-2450 • *Fax:* 44-20-3675-2451 • www.hayhouse.co.uk

Published and distributed in the Republic of South Africa by:
Hay House SA (Pty), Ltd., P.O. Box 990, Witkoppen 2068
info@hayhouse.co.za • www.hayhouse.co.za

Published in India by: Hay House Publishers India,
Muskaan Complex, Plot No. 3, B-2, Vasant Kunj, New Delhi 110 070
Phone: 91-11-4176-1620 • *Fax:* 91-11-4176-1630 • www.hayhouse.co.in

Distributed in Canada by:
Raincoast Books, 2440 Viking Way, Richmond, B.C. V6V 1N2
Phone: 1-800-663-5714 • *Fax:* 1-800-565-3770 • www.raincoast.com

✦ ✦ ✦

ACCESS NEW KNOWLEDGE.
ANYTIME. ANYWHERE.

Learn and evolve at your own pace from the world's leading experts.

www.hayhouseU.com

Hay House Podcasts
Bring Fresh, Free Inspiration Each Week!

Hay House proudly offers a selection of life-changing audio content via our most popular podcasts!

Hay House Meditations Podcast

Features your favorite Hay House authors guiding you through mediations designed to help you relax and rejuvenate. Take their words into your soul and cruise through the week!

Dr. Wayne W. Dyer Podcast

Discover the timeless wisdom of Dr. Wayne W. Dyer, world-renowned spiritual teacher and affectionately known as "the father of motivation". Each week brings some of the best selections from the 10-year span of Dr. Dyer's talk show on HayHouseRadio.com.

Hay House World Summit Podcast

Over 1 million people from 217 countries and territories participate in the massive online event known as the Hay House World Summit. This podcast offers weekly mini-lessons from World Summits past as a taste of what you can hear during the annual event, which occurs each May.

Hay House Radio Podcast

Listen to some of the best moments from HayHouseRadio.com, featuring expert authors such as Dr. Christiane Northrup, Anthony William, Caroline Myss, James Van Praagh, and Doreen Virtue discussing topics such as health, self-healing, motivation, spirituality, positive psychology, and personal development.

Hay House Live Podcast

Enjoy a selection of insightful and inspiring lectures from Hay House Live, an exciting event series that features Hay House authors and leading experts in the fields of alternative health, nutrition, intuitive medicine, success, and more! Feel the electricity of our authors engaging with a live audience, and get motivated to live your best life possible!

Find Hay House podcasts on iTunes, or visit www.HayHouse.com/podcasts for more info.